AMERICAN LIVES | Series editor: TOBIAS WOLFF

Just Breathe Normally

PEGGY SHUMAKER

UNIVERSITY OF NEBRASKA PRESS | LINCOLN AND LONDON

Lines from "Otro Mas," are from *El Corazón Amarillo*, by Pablo Neruda. Copyright 1974 Fundación Pablo Neruda. Used by permission of Fundación Pablo Neruda. English translation: Lines from "Another One," are from *The Yellow Heart*, translated by William O'Daly. Copyright 1990 by William O'Daly. Used by permission of Copper Canyon Press.

Lines from "Oda a Los Calcetines," are from *Nuevas Odas Elementales*, by Pablo Neruda. Copyright 1956 Fundación Pablo Neruda. Used by permission of Fundación Pablo Neruda. English translation: Lines from "Ode to My Socks," are from *Neruda and Vallejo* (Beacon Press, 1971), edited and translated by Robert Bly. Used by permission of the editor.

Lines from "Sixty," "Before the Sky Darkens," "After," and "A Post Mortem Guide" are from *Different Hours*, by Stephen Dunn. Copyright 2000 by Stephen Dunn. Used by permission of W.W. Norton, Inc.

Lines from "Anniversary Sonnet" are from *Days of Awe* (Copper Canyon Press, 1989), by Maurya Simon. Used by permission of the author.

Lines from "For the Anniversary of My Death," are from *The Lice* (Macmillan, 1967) by W. S. Merwin. Copyright 1967 by W. S. Merwin. Used by permission of the Wylie Agency.

Lines from "The Purpose of Altar Boys" are from *Whispering to Fool the Wind* (Sheep Meadow Press, 1982), by Alberto Ríos. Used by permission of the author.

Additional acknowledgments for previously published material appear on pages vii–ix.

∞

Library of Congress Cataloging-in-Publication Data
Shumaker, Peggy.
Just breathe normally / Peggy Shumaker.
  p. cm. — (American lives)
ISBN 978-0-8032-1095-0 (cloth : alk. paper)
1. Shumaker, Peggy. 2. Cycling accident victims — Alaska — Biography. 3. Convalescence — Psychological aspects.
4. Reminiscing — Therapeutic use. I. Title.
  RC1045.P78S48 2007   362.197'10092 — dc22
  [B]   2006101195

Set in Bembo. Designed by A. Shahan.

FOR JOE

∞

In memory of my parents
HANNA ZOE MOEN
June 12, 1933 – February 2, 1969
  and
JOHN MARSHALL HOWE
January 3, 1932 – November 2, 2006

Acknowledgments

Material from this book, sometimes in different forms, previously appeared in the following publications. Many thanks to the editors, publishers and staff members who welcomed my work:

JOURNALS
Alaska Quarterly Review, The American Poetry Review, Ascent, Bellingham Review, Blackbird, Brevity, Hayden's Ferry Review, Iowa Review, Iowa Woman, The James River Review, The Louisville Review, Manoa, Nimrod, Phoebe, West Branch

"The Apple" first appeared in verse form in *The Agni Review* 13 (1980).

"Camouflage" first appeared in *The Gettysburg Review* 15, no. 3 (Fall 2002), and is reprinted here with the acknowledgment of the editors.

"The Inside Story" first appeared in verse form in the *Women's Review of Books* 16, no.3 (December 1998).

"Just This Once" first appeared in *Crab Orchard Review* 8, no. 1 (Fall/Winter 2002).

"Landfraud Nosebleed" first appeared in verse form in *Crazyhorse* 61 (Spring 2002).

"Naming What We Hold In Our Hands" first appeared in verse form in *The Seattle Review* 28, no. 1.

"You Should Know Better" is reprinted from *Prairie Schooner* 78, no. 1 (Spring 2004) by permission of the University of Nebraska Press. Copyright 2004 University of Nebraska Press.

ANTHOLOGIES

A Road of Her Own, edited by Marlene Blessing (Fulcrum, 2002), *Looking North*, edited by Aldona Jonaitis (University of Washington Press, 1998), *Short Takes: Brief Encounters with Contemporary Nonfiction*, edited by Judith Kitchen (Norton, 2005), *Trappings: Stories of Women, Power, and Clothing*, edited by Tiffany Ludwig and Renee Piechocki (Rutgers University Press, 2007), *This Delicious Day: 65 Poems*, selected by Paul B. Janeczko (Orchard Books/Grolier, 1987), *Under Northern Lights*, edited by Frank Soos and Kesler Woodward (University of Washington Press, 2000)

BOOKS

Blaze (Red Hen Press, 2005), *The Circle of Totems* (University of Pittsburgh Press, 1988), *Esperanza's Hair* (University of Alabama Press, 1985), *Underground Rivers* (Red Hen Press, 2002), *Wings Moist from the Other World* (University of Pittsburgh Press, 1994)

Thank you to the doctors, nurses, and staff of Fairbanks Memorial Hospital.

Thank you to my whole family.
Thanks to Ginny Draves, Sue Montoya, and John Howe, my siblings who shared much of this story.
Special thanks to Amy Nettles and Hanna Cordova, the avenging nieces.
Thank you to John Howe, my father, and to Connie Howe, his wife.
Thank you to the Usibelli clan.

Many people helped during my healing. Thanks to everyone who brought food, flowers, music, poems, stories.

For help with the spelling of words in Norwegian, thanks to Professor Claudia Berguson.

Thank you to the capable and highly professional staff of the University of Nebraska Press.

Thanks always to my students.

For their sustaining friendship, thanks to Marion Baker, Christianne Balk and Karl Flaccus, Steve Berg, Marlene Blessing, Jennifer Brice, Derick Burleson, Anne Caston, Stephen Dunn, Jim and Karla Elling, Kate Gale and Mark Cull, Cynthia Hogue and Sylvain Gallais, Aldona Jonaitis, Margo Klass, Bill and Eloise Kloefkorn, Connie and Steve Kuusisto, Jan and David Lee, Susan McInnis and Joy Morrison, John and Nancy Morgan, Paul Morris and Becky Ross, Naomi Shihab Nye, Ed Ochester, W. Scott Olsen, Hilda Raz, Tito, Lupita, and Joaquín Ríos, Rachel Rose, Stan Rubin, Eva Saulitis and Craig Matkin, Glen and Melissa Simpson, Sherry Simpson and Scott Kiefer, Maurya Simon and Robert Falk, Carol Houck Smith, Ron Spatz, Virginia and Mark Spragg, Carol Swartz, Susan Thierman, Kes and Missy Woodward.

Four trusted readers helped me shape this book:
Ladette Randolph, who saw a "long essay" and kindly informed me I had a lot more to write.
Frank Soos, who read fragments early on.
Dawn Marano, who helped me with clarity and precision.
Judith Kitchen, who suggested an order for this book that would never have occurred to me.

Thanks beyond measure to Joe Usibelli.

Porque mi historia se duplica
cuando en mi infancia descubrí
mi depravado corazón
que me hizo caer en el mar
y acostumbrarme a submarino.

PABLO NERUDA, from "Otro Mas"

∞

The story of my life repeats itself —
as a small child I discovered
my corrupted heart,
which tumbled me into the sea
and accustomed me to life underwater.

PABLO NERUDA, from "Another One"
from *The Yellow Heart* translated by
William O'Daly

Just This Once

Once, in a wild place, I felt myself quiet down. I listened, drew silent breaths. It was dangerous not to warn the bears I was there, no question. But I wanted to live one moment in a wild place without disturbing the other creatures there. This delicate moment laced with fear — a life wish.

Just this once, I told myself. Everyone else snored. Black nets billowed, let in a few mosquitoes. I snuck out, careful to prop shut the cabin door so porcupines wouldn't be tempted, pulled on hip waders folded knee-high, headed up the path not singing, not calling out, not jangling bells to warn the one who left tracks bigger than ours at the edge of the water and her spring cub who dawdled behind, clawing up storm clouds of silt. Undisturbed and not disturbing, I stood still breathing in sphagnum's mossy sigh quiet after loon calls, followed unmarked paths left by stars too wild to show themselves anywhere but here, inhaled her nursing musk, the bear I knew was there.

∞

Death can come at any time. I know that.

So why was I so shocked when on a sunny Alaskan afternoon near the end of the twentieth century, near the end of a twenty-mile bike ride I damn near bought the ranch, headed for the last roundup, kicked the bucket, cashed in my chips? I almost said hey to St. Peter, shuffled off this mortal coil, heard a fly buzz, left the mirror clear.

I always figured I'd get old. So how does "any time" apply, I mean, to me? I assumed I'd sprinkle marigolds in a path for the dead to follow on Día de los Muertos, so my mother, gone in her thirties, could walk beside her mother, frail in her eighties, who told me the hardest thing in her long life—outliving two children.

∞

FAIRBANKS, JUNE 19, 2000

Three canoes drift the Chena. From our garage, we watch them round the bend in the river and slip out of sight. We strap on our helmets, zero out the last ride's numbers on the handlebar computers. It's my turn to choose where we'll pedal. Joe likes to snake through downtown or to meander through neighborhoods. I prefer less traffic and suggest, "Let's do Farmer's Loop, on the bike path where it's safe." That's fine with Joe, proud these days to be fit enough for twenty miles of hills. We pull on gloves with no fingertips and pedal off.

If you sent away for a glorious Alaskan day, this one you'd pay extra to have delivered. This afternoon splendid as the cover of a seed catalog—better even, because it sprouts on its own, a volunteer, wild gift. No effort's required of us. All we have to do is savor it.

4

The river ice is long gone, the birch trees in full leaf. Beavers gnaw 360s around trunks, then like playground bullies push down scrawny trees.

A few blocks through Hamilton Acres and we catch the bike trail along the Steese Highway. We dodge broken glass behind Big Daddy's Barbecue, dodge fireweed poking through asphalt cracks by Seekins Ford. We slalom around potholes in the dips and rills along Old Steese. Then we gear down for the wide half-mile curve that opens onto the Loop, get ready to stand on the pedals. They're deceptive, those gradual long inclines. You think you can pace yourself and make it fine, but breath tells you exactly where your limits are.

I break a sweat before we hit the collapsed place outlined in hot pink spray paint, clunk into a lower gear, and spin my legs faster, teetering a little as the hill gets serious. I aim for the crest, inhale the aroma of wet fireweed. Up top, Joe grins. Birch and spruce shade us. Then, nose down, we take on momentum. Wind we create ourselves cools our brows. We don't need to pedal almost until the Dog Musher's Hall.

We pass the odd lot where some guy (the owner? a squatter?) has nailed up stuffed animals. Hundreds of stuffed animals. Bears and cats and floppy puppies all over trees and trellises. Branches of beanie babies, pyramids of gargantuan carnival animals. He's made a forest of blue dogs, Tasmanian devils, Tweety, Sylvester, Oscar the Grouch. Blue plastic tarps crackle, the nailer's shelter. A huge yellow sign, swiped from a construction site, says, "Absolutely No Hiring." Another, "No Visitors." I pedal a little faster past his lair.

We speed up on the downhill, past the trail to our secret blueberry patches, past the pond, past the road to see musk oxen, past the back entrance to University of Alaska Fairbanks. We wait for the signal at University and College, then push on to Geist, where the bike path's fenced all the way along the side by Johansen Expressway. The other side's open sometimes, but fenced where a steep slope or the slough might be dangerous.

We breathe deeply, and feel virtuous with twenty new miles on our odometers. It's the peculiar self-congratulation of the not particularly athletic, once we get off our duffs and do something active. We laugh, the sun warm on our shoulders, a gray camp robber leading us on in glancing loops.

All along the rock meadow separating Aurora Motors from Noyes Slough we've got clear sailing. Concrete and chain link separate us from the freeway on the right. Joe has drawn a little ahead as we near the Overpass to Nowhere. Some highway planner had projected a walkway over the freeway, and the rise was added, but the path, fenced off, leads to open air.

We strain up the last big hill before the flat mile home. Joe's lead is increasing, so I pedal on the downhill, catching up. Concrete and chain link line both sides of the trail up ahead where the trees get thick. Alders grown bushy along the slough push through the fence and block the view.

༄

What comes next, I learn from Joe, again and again.

Around the blind curve comes a kid, screaming illegally down the bike path on his four-wheel ATV. Joe sees him, thinks, "Oh, man, this is gonna hurt." The ATV's suspension catches Joe's front tire, crushing it rim to hub, twisting. Joe flies over his handlebars, over the kid and the four-wheeler, and lands on his knees on the path. "Wasn't so bad," Joe thinks.

He jumps up, cursing the dumb son of a bitch, and runs to where I am lying. I'm curled on my side, back to the concrete. Both sides of my helmet are gouged and scraped. My right knee bleeds around imbedded gravel. A little trickle of blood leaks from my lips. Joe tries to get some response, but I am out.

Witnesses stop right away and call 911. A man leaps the fence and holds my head.

The ambulance can't drive all the way to where we are, so it eases out across the gravel. Then paramedics have to hoof it. Two people hold my head still as they strap me to a backboard.

I open one eye but the sun's too bright.

While he talks to police, Joe watches paramedics tending me, then sees that they're heading for the ambulance. He tries to run, to keep up, and feels his back seize.

∽

I'm under a door covered with sandbags. Muddy water's rising. My hips sink deeper into muck. I can't open my eyes until I know what's in this water. The weight crushing my chest grows heavier. Am I wearing armor? My lungs fill with wet concrete.

∽

Next thing I know, Joe's holding my foot. We're in a large room. Many people. He comes up beside me and says loving words. Then he says, "Nobody knows how to take out your contacts. Think you can do it?" (Later Joe tells me how they cut off my clothes, snipped right through the front of my bra, stuffed the scraps into a plastic bag with a handle and absurdly presented it to him.)

Things are moving fast. Flat on the gurney on the way to surgery, I open one eye. Nobody knows how to help this time. I reach up deftly with my left hand and pluck out what brings the blurry world into focus.

I close my eyes, slip backwards into the blur as wheels beneath me begin to roll.

∽

I wake in a body I barely recognize. My head's too heavy for my neck. I can't turn my face. The room swirls. It occurs to me that I must be alive. Nobody has ever mentioned that death hurts this much. My belly's bandaged, as is my right leg. My whole upper

7

body feels rubbery, numb. Joe tells me we had a wreck, on our bikes. Joe tells me not to move.

∽

It takes months of telling, Joe finding words again and again. Joe dredges up detail after detail, over and over. It takes months before my mind can see these nuggets not as separate chunks, but as part of one vein, as story.

ONE

Constants

For forty-odd years of my life, I could count on three constants: reading, writing, and the love of my mother's mother. Grandma Moen read to me, wrote to me. She thought of me every day. She let me know that anything I wrote she would read, even the painful parts. She taught me to read by reading every hour, every day.

Now she's gone from this earth. My eyes can't focus. It's as if I've just been born. Who am I? Who can I be?

Easter, Grave Tending

Just after milking, Hanna Loften tied back her skirts and knelt among the lettered stones, seven generations in need of her thick wrist twisting nettles, scraping back winter's scrim, her stiff bristles scouring themselves to nubs against chiseled names shed by those held close in stories, shed too by those forgotten. Hanna Loften rinsed and weeded till one clear star rose, the churchyard's constellations spiraling around her, fading as dawn lifted night from her eyes, one star outshining the great blazing arc Viking longboats steered by.

Stars bright at noon, just not given to us then. Evening she whipstitched edges of openwork, hardanger holes spaced evenly as graves, their beauty outlining what's no longer there.

Dovetails

My grandfather John Moen never forgave his own father. His mother, Hanna Loften, died young. Not in childbirth, not from malnutrition. She had what in those days women didn't mention to men—"female troubles." Her husband, paying off his passage, refused to call the doctor. Hanna grew so weak a neighbor offered to take her to town. "It'll be too much for her, I think," Engebret said. End of subject. End of Hanna.

John watched his mother suffer, watched her yellow, watched her writhe. He snuck in the midwife when his father was out of sight.

"She's in a bad way, son. You need to get her to town." The woman might as well have said, "You need to get her to the moon." He made his mother tea. He held her head when she leaned over the edge of the bed.

He planed the boards, fit the dovetails tight.

Vinstra

John Moen thought of his mother's folks. No word for months now. Did they have enough to eat? Had they been put off the land?

Since childhood, it had been his mother's job to clear the family plot in Vinstra, in the Gudbrands Valley of Norway. Who would care for his mother's little patch of America outside of Rocklake, North Dakota?

Lefse

Bachelor cook, he floured the board, rolled out lefse made of
last night's boiled spuds, watched brown patches rise across their
faces as if they were loved ones left behind in a country that
speaks his language.

Churning, 1924

Long before she stood at the counter of the cream station in a rubber apron, skimmed up a sample for the centrifuge, whirled it, slipped in two drops of ruby oil, set the points of calipers just so, careful as a snake balancing an egg on its fangs, delicate, the farmer watching, not that he didn't trust E. J.'s daughter you understand, but business is business and butterfat determines how many sacks of flour and meal go home in that wagon and whether or not a few yards will unwind from the bolt of muslin, new cloth for Easter, fresh skirt for his wife's made-over go-to-meeting dress and the good part of the old skirt whipped up into a waistcoat for the baby, before that, before prices she quoted let Harriet know whose skinny cow wouldn't make it through another Dakota winter, and whose skinny kids wouldn't have a baked potato to bring to school, before all that she had one big chore—butter.

After her father milked, and set tall cans in the pantry, it was her job to scoop off risen cream with a slotted spoon, slip it into a half gallon mason jar, and shake. Forever. Shake steady, shake long, shake till her arms fell off. First she'd slosh white water, rapids foaming, then watch storm clouds thundering, then witness the miraculous conception—gold, arising via her muscles, her shaking, her will—flecks to clumps to a solid chunk, new body luscious, prepared to anoint hot bread, huge farm bowls of mashed potatoes, legions of string beans. Whatever the seven sisters, their parents, and the hired hands couldn't eat, she got to sell.

What did she save her pennies for? Crank and a paddle—a mail-order churn.

Dakota's Not Gudbrandsdalen

After a full night fiddling four straight sets, after catching Harriet Langley's spitfire eye following his fingers, his bow, after hiding bootleg pints in hollows and burls of birch then selling the maps, John Moen slipped back into his bunk. One last sip and he'd sleep an hour, maybe two, before hitching the bull to the stoneboat and driving out past the slough to the north forty where more rocks than crops poked through the dust.

Three more months. With his passage paid, he could save for lessons, for airtime, could save enough to fly. Maybe set a little aside for those blue glass beads in Hawkinson's window. Maybe barter a hard week of rigging biplanes for an hour or two in the sky.

The Thing to Do

At eighteen, Harriet Langley, second daughter of a state legisla-
tor and a town leader, married John Moen, a thirty-year-old
Norwegian immigrant. What was the attraction, I asked.

"Well, he was tall, . . ." she smiled. "He made me laugh. And
he played the fiddle at the dances my father had forbidden me
and my sisters to attend. Of course any time we went, a dozen
people told on us before we got home. Anyway, John was full of
life. Those blue eyes, they sparkled."

When I asked him why they married, Grandpa grinned. "Your
mother was on the way. We thought it was the thing to do."

Milk, 1932

Spoiled, his sisters whispered, spoiled town girl who never learned to milk, who snuggled down under covers while John Moen lit the kitchen stove, then laced up work boots and tramped to the barn.

Calm Norvella never needed halter or stanchion. Eyes closed, she sighed, relieved, his chapped hands stripping two strands at a time, galvanized zings foaming.

And Harriet, new farm wife stretching in bed, massaged bag balm into the just-seen planet orbiting the milky way of her gown, homemade secret they could keep only a little while longer.

∞

Were you afraid, I asked her, my mother's mother, who once was eighteen and pregnant and out on the farm near Perth, North Dakota.

"I just figured everything would turn out all right. And pretty much, it has," Grandma said calmly.

Back Then

Back then rivers all had water in them, water we could drink. Back then, chicken coops behind the pepper tree squawked into uproar if we bounced a ball off the boards. Back then, Grandpa Moen wore work shoes grubby as fresh-dug spuds, and nipped in the bud peppers gone gangly. Back then, he could mend anything we dragged home.

Back then, he slurped risengrynsgrøt, spread on his lefse smør so thick his teeth left tracks. Back then, he chased us with limburger. Back then, he scoured us with whiskery kisses. Back then, we'd polka on top of his stocking feet, champagne bubbles rising. Back then, his boo-di-oooh-di-ooooh-di deepened any dark, shook screams out of us. Back then, Norway stuck in his throat. Over mugs of stout black coffee sucked through lump sugar, his eyes, bright blue, traveled back.

Back then, the littlest bukken bruse always made it over the bridge, made it past the hungry trollet to graze on sweet grass in high seter.

My Father's Wives #1

In lust with the whole world, my parents squirmed out of their clothes. Their teenaged bodies crashed magnificently against one another, surf undercutting the cliff where they lay. Sex was clumsy, new, unbelievable. They went at it as if they'd just invented it.

They went together like beach sand in an open eye.

They only married because I was on the way. I figured that out early. They drove to Yuma, where a new hatch of crickets writhed, a jumpy carpet, tobacco juice brown. My father's footsteps crunched and slid. Their witness, Aunt Analise, was wearing new shoes, chunky white platform heels with eyelet cutouts showing her nylons. She didn't want to get out of the car.

"Whatd'ya think, they'll crawl up and get your woolybooger?" Uncle Don poked at her. The four of them woke up the justice of the peace.

When the parents' screams pierced another midnight, my stomach clenched. All my fault, their misery.

    ∞

To judge by her scrapbook, Mom had lots of boyfriends, lots of attention. First child, first daughter. Bright and bold, ready to take on the world.

When she came up pregnant, she expected my dad to step up. And he did. They married. He worked a series of day jobs he hated. To keep his soul alive, he worked dance jobs at night. He made himself as scarce as he could, pointing to his role as the man of the house, the worker, to explain why he wasn't there (even when he was in the house), why he had nothing really to bring home, no reason really to come home.

We grew around the empty place his absence left in the family. When he was in the house, everybody felt crowded. It felt like having company that hadn't called first.

∞

I can imagine how at first, she liked his silence, her new husband who never talked. She talked all the time, a running river of words, working her way downstream till she had a better idea where she was and what she thought. She talked all the time, just to keep the conversation lively. She talked. Talked and talked.

Before long, it hurt that he never asked her even one question. Didn't he want to know her? Didn't he care what she was thinking?

Her talking crowded him. His silence let her know she was abandoned. Nobody wanted to respond. Nobody paid attention. Nobody listened.

"Mother's First Words After the Birth"

Because I was her first, no one listened when my mother cried, "It's time, it's coming!" The nurses patted her hand, crossed their legs.

"We'll tell *you*, honey, when it's getting close."

So I was almost born between floors, my mother clamping shut her thighs, some panicky orderly pinning her shoulders to the gurney. My father, a lanky teenager dreaming of a shovel-head Harley with a suicide clutch, paced.

When we were mopped up, presentable, he slouched in, reached afraid to touch my mother's flattened, baby-fine hair. His hands felt enormous, charming, full of forgiveness.

Face to the wall, my mother spoke from far away.

"I'm sorry it isn't a boy for you, honey."

∞

Imagine being the woman who would think, just after giving birth for the first time, that. Imagine her saying it out loud to her young man. Imagine her writing it down in the baby book.

The Apple

Mother slices the apple without sawing, twirls out the blossom end, the seeds, with one crisp swipe. Cross-sectioned womb, one for me, one for sister. Mother with one hand open and one fist clenched.

Hearing Voices

Little enough to climb onto somebody's lap, I love the way people's voices change when they pick up a book. Music lives in my grandma, my mom, many kinds of music. Can they hear those voices when they hold books open for hours, books with no pictures? How do they know how the animals sound, animals who can talk? Why do they hide this music? Why do they let their many voices sing only when the page is open?

Freestyle, Backstroke, Breaststroke, Butterfly

Just as my feet leave the diving board, my mother thinks to herself, "Where's that little girl's mother?" And then she realizes *she's* the little girl's mother.

Water is so much my element that any pool or puddle I see, I run over and jump in. I'm three and a half. My parents arrange swimming lessons. The lessons take place early, early, before anyone else is up, early enough so most of the kids complain, "*It's too cold.*" Not me. I wake everybody before light, so we won't be late.

The lessons happen just after sunrise, before the one-handed swim teacher has to go to work. Mike Chernis wears a hook to work, but at the pool he wears his bare stump. At my fourth birthday party, he slips nickels between the claws of his hook and lets kids keep any coins they're brave enough to come pluck out.

Double

We lived in El Cajon, California, next door to my mother's parents. I had full run of two houses and permission to go up the hill to the little store at the end of the block. I'd round up nickels and go buy chocolate Kits, those little square candies wrapped together in threes. They were perfect—one for me, one for Ginny, one for Sue. John was too little to get any.

My constant companion was a brown baby doll. I don't know if I picked her out myself, made a scene until they bought her for me. I don't know if my grandma brought her home, or if my mom gave her to me just to irritate my dad. I can imagine my dad, distressed, asking, "Where'd she get that nigger baby?" I know I never chose it, never made it up, but that name stuck.

I made up songs to sing to her, showed her the pictures in my favorite books. She was better than an imaginary friend. I looked in her eyes and told her my secrets. She listened, no matter how soft my whisper. She never told.

I fought to take Nigger Baby everywhere with me, including into the tub. If I got scolded, she did too. My mother told me later that she cringed to think she sounded like that. When I had to, I whipped her good and threw her in the trash. I fished her out when I got over it. My alter ego, doppelganger, soul sister.

She told me her stories. That's how it started. People my whole life have been trusting me with their stories.

∽

In high school, when I wanted to hang out with friends, some black, some Mexican, my dad said, "People will call you a nigger lover."

"So?" I said.

He grounded me.

I made plans.

Costumes

I was four, Ginny two. My mom made us Halloween costumes that year, clown costumes. One color on the right side, one on the left. Ginny's body was purple and yellow, mine brown and orange. The edges of our ruffs she trimmed in bias tape. On top of our soft cone hats, jingle bells. In that suit, for the first time, I could be funny. When I did a somersault, then whipped off my hat, people laughed. Ginny caught the spirit, and before long we were demented—nightmare clowns unpacked from our little car. Ginny would not let go of her golf club, even though I pointed out that it didn't go with her outfit. She told me lots of clowns play golf.

My mother stopped saying for a little while, "Peggy doesn't say much, but when she does, it counts." I never figured out if that was the way she saw me, or if that was the way she wanted me or herself to be. Anyway, for one short season, people really laughed, when I meant for them to.

Not much later, I wanted to put on my clown self again. I stepped into the costume, but couldn't pull the zipper shut. There in the closet, on a wire hanger, the too-small suit lost its power.

Egg Tooth

"This is how you hold something you love," Mom said, opening her palm till the skin pulled shiny and hard, then easing off till her hand made a little trough. The new chick snuggled down, nestling in its own softness. "You can't close your fingers or it'll struggle to get away. If you hold it too tight, you can kill it, even if you don't mean to."

The chicks put their heads back to swallow one eyedrop at a time.

We swallowed, ready to try. We practiced, hands open, newly hatched. Scaly little clawed toes sharpened themselves against our palms, the pointy mouths poking for triangle-shaped scoops of feed.

Elden

Under the drooping canopy of Grandpa Moen's pepper tree, Elden Clemmons ambushed me. He burst through the graceful branches and pinned me against shredded bark. I could feel peppercorns pressing into my back like pop beads. He planted a gushy lip-locker on my thrashing face.

"Now we have to get married!" he crowed.

What?! I was worried. Elden was in second grade and knew things I didn't because I didn't go to school yet. I shoved him off, and told him we could talk about it after lunch. Over peanut butter on Wonder bread I stewed. Fatso Elden wasn't mean, but he wasn't very smart. I could run faster than he could. I could read faster than he could, and harder books, too. I ought to get a vote, at least.

I went to Grandma Moen, found her shoving clean sheets through the wringer of her old Maytag, brought all the way from North Dakota when she moved to California. That was during the war, when metal was scarce. Her Uncle Nels had a washer in his store. She clerked for him to pay for it. When Grandpa Moen left Rocklake to build planes for Convair, Nels told Grandma, "That's the last you'll see of him."

"Grandma, what does it mean, 'have to' get married?" I asked, aiming mashed cloth better into wicker.

"Where did you hear that?" she asked. Her eyebrows arched over her glasses.

"Elden."

"Who was he talking about?"

"Me and him."

Grandma blinked, then barked out a big laugh. "You're not marrying Elden Clemmons, Peg. Don't worry."

Whew. That was close.

I climbed the mulberry tree and stayed hidden the whole afternoon, reading Little Golden Books, sun sneaking through the leaves.

Wringer

Grandma Moen's round washer teetered, spun wheel-deep in sloshed suds, garage floor not so greasy anymore. That wringer spit buttons like watermelon seeds. Blued sheets mashed flat—that washer stuck out and stuck out its tongue. Never done.

She was laughing, leaning back to grab her mug of strong black Folger's.

A wayward fold snagged her wrist, fed her fingers, hand, forearm between hard rollers. Her face bleached out. Eyes flush with rinse water, she reached and reached—the release just inches too far.

Far away, the bones in her arm spread. Exiled from this body, she watched her hem unravel. Beyond her yet, this mending.

Beaded Belt, Mt. Rushmore

Volkswagen packed tight as a tick on a boxer's dog's flop ear, we
set out toward the Black Hills, then Rocklake, North Dakota,
the mythical place my mother was born, and where she lived in
the time before time began. Five of us, mashed in that Beetle.
We stopped because it was good for us at a place so scary that
faces took the places of cliffs and canyons. We stared up Lincoln's
nostrils as long as we could, felt the hubris of humans carving
mountains in their own images.

We were little enough to whine and expect something to
come of it. A narrow belt, beaded with crude thunderbirds, my
grandma paid for. I slipped it through the loops on jeans new
enough to have complete knees, and ran around yelling.

Cinched, I rambled into scrub brush. A broken branch snagged
me, caught a few threads—broadcast colors—flecks, pierced seeds
of shame rained around my shoes.

I was little enough to cry, practicing on small losses for ones I
had no way to see coming.

A tired man on display in a full-feathered headdress spotted
me, clinked over in shell armor to pick me up, dust me off. I
saw his hand, bark-colored, brush off of me bits of Washington,
Jefferson, Roosevelt, Lincoln.

Morning Ritual

Wash my face, brush my teeth, moisten my waist-length hair
so sparks have to fly elsewhere, static crackling inside my skull.
Mom brushes us, each girl settled between her knees, brushes
hard and pulls up a ponytail so tight our eyes slit like coin slots.
Love pulls hard at the temples, leaves us raw at the nape.

Somewhere in history our ancestors had it harder, saving up to
buy nails, scrounging Norwegian forests for a few wild bites.

Their hunger flows through my mother's gathering hand,
loops around us like the rubber band, doubled, doubled again.

Diplomacy

In kindergarten, we had a sharing circle. Lots of kids were excited to tell about the Mother Goose Parade, which characters they shook hands with, how much candy they got tossed from the floats. A horse had reared right near us, a palomino with white sidewalls around both eyes. That scared animal came down hard, front hoof on the arm of a Little Miss Muffet. She dropped her tuffet, held her elbow, cried.

Two boys told how a horse got away, how it trampled six people and two died.

I turned this over and over in my mind. Then I said quietly, "We didn't go to the same parade, I guess."

Ladybugs

Quarts of ladybugs scraped off the grapevines stir and moil in mayonnaise jars. Here's luck crawling all over itself. We watch the red and black kaleidoscope until Grandpa's shoes scrape on the porch and the screen door slams. He squats down to wire-brush our cheeks, hums a hum Leet-dee-deet-de-doo Norwegian. Still crusted with dirt, his shoes boom like monster potatoes. His shoes make things right. When Lawrence and Welk staggered and their whiskers lay still in the shoebox, those shoes walked them out under the walnut trees and kicked the shovel into the ground. But this time they stride like church shoes while he shakes the jars gently, takes them outside. We hear the lids unscrew and the wings whisper. He mumbles a few words and they rise in unison, a small tornado, that quart of spirit.

Letter Carrier, 1957

To keep him out of jail and off that cursed motorcycle, Grandpa
Howe got his youngest son, Johnny, on with the post office, Point
Loma, set him up sweet, substituting, so he wouldn't by God
have any excuse—*how* could it be boring, a different route every
day? Showed Johnny tricks, like how to lean into the leather
strap, save your shoulder, or how to walk up hills backwards till
your calves got the drill.

But all John could see was Rosecrans Cemetery, row after row
of permanent addresses, stark white markers military as sharks'
teeth worn dull by sand and sea. He lasted six months. One
good Friday, he took a look at stacks taller than he was, six foot
six, obelisks of *Life* magazines, life he had to carry, deliver, pay
for with his own human sweat, falling always short of his father's
celestial visions. Squinting, his father looked at his last son side-
ways, as if the light hurt his eyes, washed out blue, the only pale
part of his sun-baked face.

John quit, wandered unstable cliffs near Torrey Pines, and listened, listened for hours with his musician's ears, listened for
ocean song, wind song. Song that would sing him into any life
on this earth he could possibly lead.

Asthma

The reason she couldn't swim, couldn't push us on swings. The reason we moved away from the sea into the desert. The reason one whole cupboard rattled with her pills. The reason palo verde in bloom sent her careening to St. Joseph's. The reason I sat close, grabbed the wheel when her lips turned blue. The reason she hugged so hard. The reason no animal found refuge in her lap. The reason she stashed vodka bottles in the ragbag. The reason she yelled, "Go to the broom closet and pick out a stick." The reason smoke filled her eyes. The reason mournful cowboy songs riddled her. The reason her first breaths in the morning scraped and clattered like rusty hay balers. The reason she couldn't carry a tune in a bushel basket with a lid. The reason she sang anyway. The reason at sunset in her throat her husband kick-started his Harley, spit gravel behind him as he peeled out. The reason her laugh—sheet lightning—cracked the sky. The reason she picked through spaghetti she didn't make herself. The reason she quit eating. The reason she loved quiet more than her own kids. The reason quiet never entered her body, never entered her mind. The reason she didn't want to be here. The reason she left. The reason we buried her breathless.

Snapshot

Grandma Moen fretted the morning my family left for Arizona, left next door and drove to a place nobody'd been. I take down from her wall the picture she snapped that morning—my dad, impatient and chafing; my mom, tired already. I'm five, holding the leash of our boxer dog, Pepi. The little kids are messing around, Ginny with one of those wheels that zips inside, outside a long metal U, up and down, not going anywhere, but making good time. I remember asking my mom if the people in Arizona would speak English.

My grandma tells me how worried she was. My mom might have an asthma attack and she'd be alone with us kids in Tucson, far away where my grandma couldn't help her. Even then Grandma could predict that my mom would spend her marriage mostly solo.

Our car broke down in the desert, and we had to leave Pepi with some guys at a gas station. I remember my folks arguing, my mom taking too long gathering up stuff for four kids and herself, my dad just digging out his own.

My grandma says, guilty, "I advised her to stay in that marriage, for you kids."

I tell her, "Maybe you can let that go now." The marriage was no picnic, for anybody, but my mom has been dead now for decades. "Depends, though. You get a bigger kick out of guilt or absolution?" Grandma smiles then, and tucks away her sorrow in its reserved place.

Babies

As a teenager, Harriet Genevieve Langley became pregnant with Hanna Zoe Moen, my mother. Hanna Zoe, as a teenager, got me. I decided, deliberately, not to take that road.

Was I wiser? Uglier? Less fertile? More restrained? Less given to impulse or passion? None of the above. I had the means, technological and otherwise, to make different choices.

I was shaped by her example: very young my mother got pregnant. She got married, had four babies and two miscarriages by the time she was twenty-four. Baby in '52, miscarriage in '53, baby in '54, baby in '55, miscarriage in '56, baby in '57.

We wrecked her life, she got divorced, she died.

She wanted more choices for me.

Besides, I was always the oldest, oldest of four kids in our family. Then when Dad married Crazy Marcia, oldest of seven. Then when he married Lola, oldest of twelve. With Bobbie, oldest of six. I was not romantic about children.

When I mentioned my reluctance to have kids to a friend, he said, "Maybe you've already done that." Well, yes. But with even less authority and control than parents have, considering I was also a kid.

At our house, the division was always clear—parents, Peggy, and the little kids. Ginny was only two years, two months, and two days younger, but I was expected to care for her and the others, expected to see to their needs, feed them, dress them, set a good example.

Having skipped my adolescence, I had it in my thirties, pushing the boundaries, packing up and taking off solo, driving from Arizona to Alaska.

I didn't want a child until I could support it myself. I watched too many women, alone via divorce or disease or disaster or dipsomania or death, too many women left to flounder, trying to keep themselves and their kids above water.

When Joe asks if I would like to make a child, I'm in my late forties. All the longing I have in that direction wells up. But no. I like my life. I like sharing the lives of my nieces and nephew, their children, Joe's grandchildren. I tell him I made that decision a long time ago.

Blazes

Wounds we inflict on white bark of a birch to show those who follow which way we passed. Cut deep enough to show us maybe the way home. White wash down the face of a sorrel mare loping toward but missing the box canyon.

Flash from the muzzles of well-oiled rifles, stocks fit to three generations of shoulders, barrels aimed always at what we bring down.

Flares in the forest, where grime-smeared fighters stoop over Pulaskis, chopping smolders out of earth, the charred ground exhaling second-hand smoke, smoke in their faces, ash settling for weeks, that bad dream you can't shake, dream of not breathing, buried, deeper than light, deeper than restless earth, deeper than spirits still passionate without bodies, deeper than any way out.

∞

He had no choice, the emergency room surgeon. He split me.
Starting the cut between my breasts, he sliced my abdomen,
took a neat detour to the left of my navel, and kept going five
more inches. At first the incision was crudely stapled together,
the edges bright red and puckered. When he pulled the staples,
the scar flattened into a shiny purple ribbon of highway, dots like
postholes along both sides. I stroke it, my new ornament, lustrous
skin delicate as iris petals.

∾

Down below, hidden in the thicket, the barely visible scratch mark left from last year's surgery—planned, controlled. Last year, I asked to see what they took out of me, curious about the organs I'd carried every second of my life but never got to see. My trusted doc said, "Of course," and brought them to me. She even took Polaroids of my innards. They weren't what I expected.

"You should know better," I told myself. But truth be told, I wanted to see. Think about how for a woman so much is tucked inside. Think about how when someone else looks closely, there's a drape between the woman and her own body. It's very foreign, even when she trusts her doctor.

Nobody, no matter how starved for touch, looks forward to a pelvic exam. Nobody sings zippedy-do-dah with her feet in stirrups, even stirrups cozied up in oven mitts.

She warms the speculum, my good doctor, warns me before each touch. And still I jump a little, push back from the edge a little, close my eyes to interrogation, no parts private under probing lights.

I try to see this as routine. Spritz fixes cells swabbed from my cervix onto glass slides, their testimonies invisible to the naked eye. One gloved hand inside she slides the warm other skin to skin over my abdomen. This year she stops. Checks again.

Waits till I dress to say to my face *Tumors*. I stutter, What b-brings them on? and she says, professional as ever, *Dirty thoughts, usually*.

Well, no wonder.

This weird cellular stuff's passed down and down, generations. Nobody in my family ever breathed a word. I call my grandmother, blurt, "What do you know about hysterectomies?" and she says, *I only had one. One's all you get, you know.*

What's the etiquette? I ask to see it, whatever they take out, curious about what has come to live in me, curious too to see in person what I've known mostly from sketches—instructions tucked inside the Tampax box, The Visible Woman, her layers peeled back, *Our Bodies, Ourselves,* and once in the '70s a practitioner's purple hand mirror held so I could see.

Groggy after surgery, thumbing the pain button like a contestant on *Jeopardy—What is morphine?*—I imagine never moving again. Each swell of pain crests, rolls on. The thread stitching me together dissolves.

Of course they found things they hadn't counted on. Of course my beloved kissed the scar.

And because I asked, they showed me my Fallopian tubes sturdy as heater hoses. My cervix knobby as a punched nose. Slashed tire womb. The tumor that grew inside heavy, a shot put, but marbled, muscular, my secret unscathed heart.

And the bonus tumor growing on a stalk, odd yellow, yolk of all my eggs never ripened into children, renegade ovary, releasing all through me fugitive colors.

∽

Terrible thirst. My mouth, nostrils, eyelids dry out. My tongue is a snake shedding its skin. The earth as far as I can see has cracked into broken shards. Desiccated husks of cicadas crunch under my bare feet. I feel my own carapace coming loose.

Water used to be here. Maybe if I dig.

∽

Coming around, one eye circling, I can't tell whether death hurts this much or whether breath this measured is a bad joke, taken in by machines. Blank spots dot my brain. Beneath staples, no spleen. What else is missing? The impact, done and gone, nowhere to be seen.

46

My own edges, sharpened by pain dulled by morphine, morphing. Long days my loved ones treaded rough water while I
floated, face down.

Ice cold lemonade I scrawl, and Joe dips the swab in ice chips. I
need to wash these smells off my body. I need to cut away the
snarled mess so my head can rest, level.

∞

I wake to Joe's voice, "Here she is!"

Where is he? He comes around the end of the bed, into my
chopped field of vision.

"What happened to us?"

I cannot hold on to any answer.

Joe tells me he's been by my side ever since we made it to the
hospital, except when they wheeled me into surgery.

"How are *you*?" I ask.

"Got some bruises I'm going to enter in the fair," Joe says.

"What happened to us?"

Joe asks what I remember.

Not much. We were coasting downhill, warm from pedaling,
cool from the wind. I almost remember someone touching my
head.

Joe says, "You never saw the kid?"

"What kid?"

∞

I watch their lips, two doctors. Two doctors I don't know. Their
lips tell me skull fracture, small strokes, collapsed lung. (Joe will
tell me many times.) They tell me splenectomy, internal injuries, bleeding. Those lips describe my degloving laceration.
Concussion. Broken finger. I lift the hand without the IV to wipe
my eyes. That's when I notice my left eye's not open. Joe touches
me. His eldest son Joe and his wife Marilyn, relieved, say, "Hi. It's
good to see you." How long have they been standing there, waiting? They don't have chairs. I wish they had chairs. I smile, fade.

⁓

Strokes. So many ways to caress this word. Whether painter's sable or flogger's lash, each slash is meant to stay, to mark the moment and to live on, bearing witness to all who see the scar, whether or not they understand where it came from, brush or bullwhip.

Bubble or clot, hard block stopping blood to the brain, blanks out territories that won't be heard from again, blanks out the middle of a sentence, the whole family of words, paints over whole passages of a marked life, memorable to those marked out, remarkable.

⁓

Officer Wellborn, of the Fairbanks Police, interviews us in the hospital, once when I am barely conscious. Joe tells his version. When I can talk, I tell him how much I don't know. No, no memory of the impact. No, I didn't see the four-wheeler coming. No, I don't remember seeing the driver.

Later a neurologist will tell me about the "lag time" between perception and when the brain files something away in memory. If trauma occurs in between, the perception won't register, or is lost to recall. So I'm spared reliving the moment of the wreck.

Living with the aftermath's plenty. One witness, the woman who called 911 from her car, works at the hospital. She stops by to see how we are and mentions that she saw the kid outrunning traffic on the Johansen Expressway moments before he hit us.

Later we get a letter from a man in Utah, a man who was vacationing in Alaska with his nine-year-old daughter, a man who jumped the fence to hold my head. Though I have a distant sense of his touch, I have no memory of his face.

His daughter, waiting in the car on the shoulder of the highway—I hate to think what she saw, the images she took home from Alaska.

⁓

48

I almost remember someone touching my eyelids, touching my head. I almost remember a voice, far away, saying, "Collar."

These sensations vibrate inside me. I have no way of sorting out whether they're invented, recalled, prompted, suggested.

∽

A family I've never met comes to the hospital to visit. The dad looks shaken, lost. The mom is scared. Of what, I wonder. The kid, about seventeen, is lanky and uncomfortable. He wants to be anywhere but here. He apologizes for hurting us, offers a card and a small gift—wind chime birds. He looks like a bird with its wings tied, struggling inside his body. He looks like he might fly right into the closed window.

∽

When nurses change the dressing, I notice two plastic bulbs shaped like heads of garlic growing from tubes coming from my body. They're draining blood after the surgery, the nurse tells me.

What tool did they use to punch holes through my body for these drains? They're coming out of unharmed patches.

Down my middle, I count twenty-six staples, one for each letter of the alphabet. What does this alphabet spell?

When they lift the gauze off my leg, more staples, another drain. Out of my right side, a tube to reinflate my lung. Out of sight, the Foley catheter.

Dangling above, two ivs. Drop, drop, drop. A single drop, unending. Some part of my mind knows that they're helping me. Another part watches, hypnotized, as each drop wears away a little of the person I used to be.

∽

Drop by drop, maybe this minute erosion will wear away sandstone and shale until a slot canyon twisted deep inside me reveals itself for the first time.

∞

How can I measure what I'm really made of, when each moment it changes?

∞

"What happened to us?"

I watch Joe draw in a deep breath. I know then I've asked and asked many times. And he has answered. He gathers himself, trying hard. What could he say that would stay heard?

∞

The day after the wreck we were supposed to be in the Brooks Range, building a walkway between our two frumpy cabins and repairing the gnawed places opened up by porcupines.

I picture getting into the Widgeon, an amphibious plane with an entry about the size of a small cupboard. Let's see—big step up, balance on the foothold, bend, lift one foot into the opening, crouch, balance, lift in the other foot. Walk bent over up to a seat near the nose. Scrunch into the seat, reach overhead and behind for the two-shouldered seatbelt. Reach up and behind for radio headsets.

After flying without a plane, we won't be flying in that one any time soon.

∞

Later, friends ask, "We visited you in the hospital, remember?" And I don't. Not one glimpse, not one detail.

How much of one life flies by . . .

Butter pecan we pass up in the name of virtue. The trail not hiked. The scent of unbought flowers. All the unnoticed moments alive inside us, hidden always, parts of us never to surface.

∞

Later, I look closer at the card. The boy who signed it didn't write the words about how sorry, how terrible, how sorry. The mom did. The dad and the kid just signed on.

⚬⚬

One day, pain's not the strongest part of me any more. I'm through that part this time. Exhausted by all we cannot know, I just want to go home. Now.

⚬⚬

Before I can go home, the doctor says I have to control my pain with pills, walk, drink, eat, and excrete. This is not exactly the "high achiever" roster of tests. But it takes many days to check them off.

When I have energy, I plot strategies for turning, practice lifting one limb at a time. Keeping still wipes me out. I notice—ouch— every time my torso makes the slightest shift. Even talking exhausts me—so much concentration just to remember who people are, people I know, people allowed in to see me in intensive care.

Sleep turns fickle. Though I'm groggy all the time and can drop off in the middle of a word, my body isn't refreshed. It's hard to rest even with too much sleep.

When an aide comes in at midnight, I've just dropped off. She tells me she needs to check vital signs and to draw blood. I snap at her. "Come back in the morning. And if I'm asleep then, don't wake me." Whatever they need to know won't be that different in a few hours.

In fact, the body in all its mystery grows even more mysterious the more we poke and prod. So many variables, so many pos- sibilities. I feel exceptionally fragile, knowing what I know.

⚬⚬

Much later I wonder who told the kid to come say he was sorry. His family? His lawyer?

⚬⚬

Straight from the ICU into a wheelchair, I celebrate being outdoors. Joe and his son Mitch wheel me to the car. We've practiced standing, practiced lowering my body into a sitting position. It's trickier in a parking lot, between the blue lines of the close spaces my injured body occupies. I feel every inch of my scar, every place they pulled out staples. Is there enough left for me to hold myself together?

TWO

∞

Constants

I think of rolling down the hills at Tucson's Himmel Park, every Saturday, after our visit to the library. My mom negotiates with the librarian for a special card so I can take out as many books as I want, and not just from the children's section. I take as many as I can carry, pile my stash in the car, and then run up and roll down, run up and roll down, flushed and sweaty and Bermuda-grass itchy, full body press with the world.

Arroyo

The best kid feature of our house at 7002 Calle Ileo was the arroyo out back. It was the social center of the neighborhood, the place kids poked their fingers to become blood brothers, the place they met for fights. The arroyo brought us things we didn't recognize. The arroyo led beyond where we were allowed to go.

At first, desert stretched from the other side of that ditch to Davis Monthan Air Force Base way off on the horizon. Nothing else.

On our living room walls, we had just three ornaments, nothing else. Three Audubon prints glassed in cheap frames, images painted not from life, but from birds shot and stuffed, posed so he could get them right. Birds shot even if they were the last known members of their species.

The Magnavox stereo was long as an empty buffet table and had rolling doors that opened horizontally. We weren't supposed to roll out the turntable without an adult present, weren't allowed to lift the diamond needle and place it on the ungrooved margin at the record's edge. We weren't supposed to bump the stereo when a record was on, weren't to dance to Johnny Mathis singing "Stranger in Paradise." Or else. My dad told us he was the one Jimmy Dean was singing about who stood six foot six and weighed two forty five, Big Ja-ohn, Big Bad John.

When my dad left for good, Mom took us to Sears and forced us to buy record albums we didn't want so she could max out the credit cards. There were lots of other things we did want. She said we didn't have time to shop. I never listened to those albums, didn't even slit the cellophane.

I waited for the parents both to be gone. I pressed my ear

against the fabric over the speaker, and let the little kids sleep while I listened alone to a faraway voice, crooning about flying down the street on the chance that we'll meet. In the song, the young lovers always meet, not really by chance. That parallel universe, where passion transforms people into beings better able to find and give and receive love.

Iron Filings

Down in the arroyo, we took our magnets, lifted metallic fur from black swaths in the sand. We filled film canisters, heavier than you'd believe, with whiskers of iron. The way each strand leapt onto our little red horseshoes let us know—the earth is full of attractions nobody can see.

Watermelon Relay

When I swim in the eight-and-under category, I worship my coach, Mr. Gil Carillo. My mom gets me a team suit, a sleek navy blue tank. Around the left strap I fasten the token that gets me in to practice. I line up one little ball on the metal chain and pull it firmly into the opening in the little metal tube.

In the locker room, I wonder why the women don't care if anybody sees them. They don't care even if they have big moles or scars or hair in weird places.

Mr. Carillo picks me to swim freestyle in the watermelon relay. That's the last leg, the most important. After the third leg, Vicki Vukovich touches the rim. I uncoil, body flat along the surface. I stroke hard, breathing over my left shoulder, my kick steady, long. After one length, I flip turn, just like Mr. Carillo taught me, push off hard from the back wall. My form's good. I can feel the water cupped in each hand streaming along my body. I give it all I've got.

Almost the whole way. Then my left side feels like somebody shoved a switchblade in it. I slow down. I stretch to touch, then lift my head. We come in second, earn the red ribbon.

Mr. Carillo is hopping up and down. "You were ahead!" he yells. "Why'd you stop?"

"It hurt," I say, thinking that easing off's a reasonable response to pain.

"Don't you want to win?"

"Not if it has to hurt."

I knew even then that pain wouldn't buy me what I need to live.

Good Bluffer

Twice a week, I played poker with the milkman. Almost every time I took his quarters. I figured I was hot stuff, prit-tee dang good. I never realized I might amuse him, might give him each morning a chance to be kind.

Moving Water, Tucson

Thunderclouds gathered every afternoon during the monsoons. Warm rain felt good on faces lifted to lick water from the sky. We played outside, having sense enough to go out and revel in the rain. We savored the first cool hours since summer hit. The arroyo behind our house trickled with moving water. Kids gathered to see what it might bring. Tumbleweed, spears of ocotillo, creosote, a doll's arm, some kid's fort. Broken bottles, a red sweater. Whatever was nailed down, torn loose. We stood on edges of sand, waiting for brown walls of water. We could hear it, massive water, not far off. The whole desert might come apart at once, might send horny toads and Gila monsters swirling, wet nightmares clawing both banks of the worst they could imagine and then some.

Under sheet lightning cracking the sky, somebody's teenaged brother decided to ride the flash flood. He stood on wood in the bottom of the ditch, straddling the puny stream. "Get out, it's coming," kids yelled. "GET OUT," we yelled. The kid bent his knees, held out his arms.

Land turned liquid that fast, water yanked our feet, stole our thongs, pulled in the edges of the arroyo, dragged whole trees root wads and all along, battering rams thrust downstream, anything you left there gone, anything you meant to go back and get, history, water so high you couldn't touch bottom, water so fast you couldn't get out of it, water so huge the earth couldn't take it, water. We couldn't step back. We had to be there, to see for ourselves. Water in a place where water's always holy. Water remaking the world.

That kid on plywood, that kid waiting for the flood. He stood and the water lifted him. He stood, his eyes not seeing us. For a moment, we all wanted to be him, to be part of something so wet, so fast, so powerful, so much bigger than ourselves. That kid rode the flash flood inside us, the flash flood outside us. Artist unglued on a scrap of glued wood. For a few drenched seconds, he rode. The water took him, faster than you can believe. He kept his head up. Water you couldn't see through, water half dirt, water whirling hard. Heavy rain weighed down our clothes. We stepped closer to the crumbling shore, saw him downstream smash against the footbridge at the end of the block. Water held him there, rushing on.

Sand Rubies

The best treasure came to us mostly after rain, when the arroyo rearranged itself to suit the wet. We'd have to kneel at least, or sit quietly for a long time. This meditation turned us into visionaries, ones who could see what lay buried not far beneath. Red glints, stones precious because they disappeared. Sand rubies. Deep red and transparent one moment, flecks diving out of sight the next. In this way, we learned to savor what is always there, especially when we can't see it. In this way we learned to love ephemera: the sand of the ancient ocean, this earth, this life, everything loaned for a brief time to us.

Bedroom

Our room, shared by three sisters, was chaos. Knee-deep dirty clothes, school papers, old magazines, shoes and toys and rocks. It smelled like a cat box because the cats just dug around for a convenient place.

Ginny slept on the top bunk, burrowed into a heap of stuffed animals. She sucked her thumb until fifth grade, and rubbed the fur off whatever kitten she could catch. One had been taken too soon from its mother, and nursed on her earlobe. She liked that. Ginny dumped out her dresser drawers so she'd have room for her rocks. She collected pretty ones until the bottoms dropped out of every flimsy drawer.

Sue slept around a steaming piss hole in her mattress, hole big enough to stuff with a grubby couch cushion she picked up in the ditch. She'd smooth an old towel over the top and climb in. Always scared, Sue stayed in her pajamas, stayed glued to the TV, even when nothing good was on. She practiced hard staying invisible. After Halloween, Sue rationed her candy, one piece a day. She tucked her stash deep in a hidey hole under her bed. Once in a while she'd share with the rest of us gluttons who'd gobbled all of ours in a few days. Rock-hard and dusty, the last pieces Sue still had at Easter.

John was youngest, the only boy. He got a room of his own. Of course he liked to sneak into ours so he wouldn't be alone. John was still pretty little when he got popped for stealing parts off another kid's bike to repair his own. The other kid's mom called the cops. The kid, crying, pointed out pieces of what used to be his bike. Two police officers spoke to my mother. Just by walking into it, they filled up our carport. With stern faces, with hands on their holsters, they discussed whether or not they should haul John to jail right now and how many years he would get. My stomach clenched. Mom was nodding. Yes, probably they should take John to jail. Tears streamed down my face. John was already as small as he could get without melting into the rutted asphalt. The policemen got a call on their radio. They told John they'd be watching him. Then they got in their car and pulled away, lights flashing.

∽

Every few months, Mom would yell, "At least clear a path!" and we'd kick and shove more junk under the bed. If she came in to inspect, we'd pretend we had actually put something away.

Once when she told us we had to stay in there until the whole thing was clean, I looked around, hopeless. Then I told Ginny and Sue, "If you clean up, I'll read to you." They liked that idea, so I read, they slaved.

Thee Hannah! I choose to read to them, the story of a young girl who envies her friend's colorful bonnet, the spray of flowers inside the brim, the satin ties sky blue. I read with expression, doing the voices of the mother, the friend, of Thee Hannah. "Get Thee behind me, Old Spotty!" she says to the devil.

Hannah spoils her new gray bonnet by pinning real flowers into the fabric, staining it with their life-juices. Her mother makes her undo them, then ties the plain bonnet under Hannah's chin.

In a back street, a family of slaves running toward freedom recognizes her as a friend, a Quaker, and asks for directions. Hannah's surprised that she knows what to do. And after that she's proud of her bonnet, its message plain.

Hanging Clothes

One hand through the waistband then through the leghole, wet
underwear fresh from the sloshing Tide piles up till Hanna's arms,
weighed down, unmentionable, take effort to hold high, voo-
doo priestess in blessing. Dress shirts and dish towels draped over
skivvies give coolness gravity. Hanna slips on rubber thongs for
the sprint to the wire, T-stands stranded five times, clothespins
splintered under Tucson's sun. Hem to hem, pied shirts spread
semaphore SOS. Rescue never comes.

The Next Summer

I practiced gliding underwater, the full length of the pool, twenty-five yards. Then two lengths, fifty yards. Then more, lungs pulsing as I made the last turn. To ease the ache, I let a little stream of bubbles go, but held most of it in.

I practiced sitting on the bottom of the pool, staying under as long as I could, eyes open to the liquid sky, my secret world quiet and cool. Underwater I could be graceful. I could glide through the world. I could walk on my hands, feeling the sun first on bare feet, then calves, then thighs, facing the deep end, traveling uphill, away.

Having Words

One recurring argument between my parents—books. For my mother, there could never be enough. For my father, if you had a shelf full of Reader's Digest Condensed Books, why did you need more? They argued about whether to invest in a *World Book Encyclopedia* or a new motorcycle.

"The encyclopedia is for the whole family," my mother said.

"I'll take the kids on rides," my father countered.

I had just received by mail order a new book about Harriet Tubman. She had the same first name as my Grandma Moen, so I could trust her. Underground railroad. I cried for the slaves, running, taking only what they could carry.

How far would I have to walk to get away? Who could I count on to guide me in the dark or the desert or the heat?

Back Dive

Practicing back dives from the side of the pool, I'm so limber, I almost skin my nose on the side as I slice down. I haul myself up, step up past the gutter, flip back again. Again. Again. I settle my toes in the hollow before the tile lip rounds, push back extra hard, trying for a little extra height. My entry's not smooth. I need to do that one over. My arms tremble as I try to get out. I swim to the steps and stagger to my towel.

Halfway home, my head hurts. I think, *Maybe my bathing cap's too tight.* I undo the strap and peel off the cap. The beach towel over my shoulders fills with blood. My scalp tightens along the base of my neck. I taste iron.

When I make it home, Mom is talking to Mrs. Roush. They turn. Mrs. Roush almost falls down, faint. Mom deadpans, "Don't bleed on the carpet."

She washes my cut in the kitchen sink, sees that it'll need stitches. We head for the emergency room, my hand clamped over my head, blood seeping between my fingers.

I hold my breath.

Biting

The biter in our neighborhood picked on Ginny. She'd come wailing home down the hill with teeth-marks, dotted ovals swelling red on her forearm. The biter was another little girl about her same age, a girl she liked to play with. So we heard in Ginny's voice both physical pain and betrayal.

My mother marched over to the monkey bars and dragged the little girl down. She said, "Hold out your arm." The girl did. "Bite her back," my mom told Ginny. Ginny looked up through her tears. She shook her head. "You have to. She has to learn. Bite her back."

Ginny mouthed the arm, insincere. "Bite her," Mom insisted. Ginny looked straight at her friend, and bit down. The girl wailed, in surprise as much as pain. She thought hard before she bit Ginny again.

Neighborhood Kids, Tucson

Nelson Roush had such big buck teeth he couldn't close his lips, even to kiss. Pam Pitzer went to the Arizona State School for the Deaf and Blind, and turned our fingers into alphabets. Then our hands sang, silently. Googie Sopher was slow, we thought, until the school sent home a note saying he couldn't hear in one ear. On summer nights, we ganged up after dark, the only time cool enough to play. Murder at Midnight, Sardines, Princess and Slaves. The buds of my breasts rubbed raw on my undershirt. Johnny Mann dragged around, never wanted to do anything. He was famous for falling asleep standing up. One summer he went to visit his grandparents. When he got back, he was a regular kid, weaned off his mama's drugs. Gary Barman's dad kept their lawn perfect as a velvet carpet. Gary could fold his toes back, then walk on the tops of his feet. His arms stretched out like the Catholics' Jesus, still on the cross. We stole looks inside their church, saw Him there, roasting over hundreds of candles flickering in red glass. Linda Geiling had a swimming pool but never invited anybody over. She leapt and twirled on the dry Bermuda grass in her front yard, a dervish in July heat. She was so flexible she could do splits right leg forward, left leg forward, both legs out to the sides. She never got to watch television at home, so at our house she would sit with her nose almost on the screen. Oblivious to the world Linda would gyrate her genitals into the rug. She ended up running away to join the Ice Capades. Really. Vicki, Robin, and Jeri Lou Watson had to go every year to the Shriners Hospital in California to get new leg braces to replace the ones they'd outgrown. Bobby Kingston found droopy, snotty balloons under the oleanders by the Catholic church. Delores

Durham got one dollar allowance *every week*. Unbelievable. She spent those dollars on single records—"Help," "Satisfaction," "Ferry Cross the Mersey," "This Diamond Ring," "Brown Eyed Girl," "Runaway." We stacked 45s on our thumbs, then slipped them as high as they would go over the big-hole spindle on her portable hi-fi. Kenny Kidwell didn't play with us any more after police found his dad in a brand new yellow convertible, shot through the head. Self-inflicted GSW. Our first suicide. Donnie, three blocks over, was the second. He was in eighth grade, and constantly practiced till he got it perfect tying a noose. Randy Fahr had bedroom eyes. He invited me swimming at his backyard pool. He tried to take off my top. When a drunk driver broke Grandpa Moen's neck, my mom sent each of us to a different neighbor so she could fly to El Cajon to be with him. I went to the Waldens' house. Kris Walden had the beautiful thick curled eyelashes models try to create with mascara. Kris and I tried walking tightrope along the footboard of her bed. I fell, straddling the wood. They couldn't stop the bleeding. Her parents took me to a strange doctor who shined a bright light between my legs, then pronounced me "intact." I curled up in the fetal position. Don Maclean, Barton Lee's dad, used to trick or treat dressed up in camo fatigues, carrying a flask. He groveled for a shot at each house. Little kids he'd scare with his full-face ogre mask—AH-NU-NA-NU-NINI! Barton Lee was an only child. She used to say to the rest of us, "You're all figments of my imagination. I'm the only one who's real. If I forget to think of you, you'll die." We played with her anyway. She had a stack of comic books as tall as I was, a whole shelf of china dogs, a microscope.

Horses

It took hours to earn the dollar fifty that it cost to ride a real horse, money we got by mucking out stables or babysitting neighbor kids. So most days, we galloped in the backyard. Satan and Diablo, Blue Devil. We didn't ride these horses. We *became* horses, sixteen hands, powerful, stamping dust. We threw back our wiry manes, flicked flies with our tails. Uncurried, hooves untrimmed, we galloped up and down the arroyo, sand holding the pattern of our trail, the shifting prints of our spirits.

The Box

The rock maple dresser was passed down to Mom. The wavy dresser mirror reflected ancestors getting ready, generations of double checking, fretting, doubts. On top of that dresser sat the box. The box we were never allowed to open. Mom kept her secret stuff inside white leatherette lined with red velvet, and only offered us a glimpse once in a long while.

I wanted one of my own, a place not for jewels (stupid), but for secrets. I wanted some secrets, and the power to keep people out.

Hints never worked. I flat out told her what I wanted. The night before my birthday, I was on my way to bed after *Chiller*, spooked a little. I glanced in the yawning door to Mom's room. She was cutting out little rectangles of hot pink felt, dotting them with Elmer's, fitting them into cubbyholes.

Damn, I thought. Green plastic, that cheap box, with a picture of two kittens embossed on the lid, kittens batting a ball of yarn. My throat burned. All her work. I was going to have to pretend to like it. I was going to have to pretend it was somehow in the same universe with what I wanted.

What kind of secrets could stay in that box?

Turquoise Dress

Just before I started fourth grade, my mom brought home from a rummage sale a little turquoise dress with puffed sleeves. The fabric, sheer as running water, cascaded over my head and baptized my body. So cool. Like wearing my own personal cloud, in a place where rain's a rare blessing. A black velvet ribbon tied around the waist. Not in back like the sashes on little-girl dresses, but in front, a touch of elegance I tied myself. I slid the bow over my left hip.

That year, my teacher Mrs. Garner opened the world of the arts to me, took time away from teaching us the exports of Brazil to have us choreograph our own dances, write and act out our own plays, put down on paper our private songs and stories.

She had as much fun as we did building the Amazon out of chicken wire and papier mâché. I spent the most time on our life-size crocodile, mixing just the right shades to paint the ivory teeth and jungle-green toenails. When he wasn't there after Christmas vacation, I was sure he had whipped his tail and torpedoed away underwater.

I wore the turquoise dress every day I could get away with it. It was the first garment I learned how to wash out by hand. Hung on a painted wire hanger (I was careful to choose one that wouldn't rust), the dress dried quick as a good laugh.

In the turquoise dress, anything could happen. I could fly to school, arriving for patrol duty before my feet even knew where we were going. I could play my stop sign like a guitar, and sing "Cielito Lindo" to the Catalina Mountains. Loitering at recess by the ramada, I would *look* ordinary, but I could be swimming with manta rays and sharks. Watching the world through my sleeve of water, I could hold my breath as long as I wanted, and live for years under the sea.

Powerful, I could walk home with Karen Pfantz, even though the other girls would make fun of us. Karen wore faded old lady dresses from the bargain bin at the Disabled Vets store. Karen got the lowest grade, always. After every test, she lifted the lid of her desk and let big drops water her notebooks. The popular girls jeered, "You don't like *Karen*, do you?"

"Just ignore them," I told her. She tried. Her horsy face gathered itself up as if she were trying to refuse the bit. We took the long way to her house, playing under the footbridges where they crossed the arroyos, getting a drink out of the Roush's hose. We wondered out loud if their lives were better in the Roush's house since Mrs. Roush painted the top half lavender. She left the bottom half bare adobe.

Eventually, though, we had to take Karen home. Her father would rouse himself out of the stupor of that day and growl. I stayed as long as I could, knowing that as long as I was there he wouldn't do to Karen what he did to her every day after school. That turquoise dress made me brave so I could stay. Then I'd go home to see if Mom was drunk or sober.

One day, Karen didn't come to school. Nobody said anything. When I asked, the nurse told me she moved to Florida.

Blessings on you, Karen Pfantz, wherever you are, I thought.

A dust devil swept the playground, and I crouched down so my turquoise dress could shield my bare legs. Red—all I could see with my eyes hidden in the crook of my elbow was red, the waxy tulip shade seen through closed lids. As I stood up after the storm, a stampede of boys headed my way from the tether-ball courts. *Ya-Ya, Ya-Ya,* they bellowed. One grabbed my sleeve, hard.

Almost slow motion, how the fabric gave way. Almost an early-morning dream, when you don't know if you're asleep or awake. The sleeve's seam held. Threads all across the back let go quietly, no great rip. Karen, never complaining. My dress hung down over my bare shoulder, my slip strap in plain sight.

Where did they come from, those big gulping sobs? I hardly ever cried, and never in front of people. Even when the bell rang, I couldn't stop. The boy, defending himself before the playground monitor, said, "Why are you so upset? It was an old dress. You wear it every day."

The playground monitor meant to console. "He only does that because he likes you, you know."

I shuffled in, huddled under my desk lid. My cloud had torn. I couldn't mend it.

Mrs. Garner took me aside, murmured, "You don't need a special dress to be powerful. It was just a reminder."

Shelter

The big argument in the prosperous houses was this: do we build a bomb shelter or a swimming pool? (We weren't getting either one, so we didn't have this fight at home.)

During the Cuban Missile Crisis we had to take home notes. Our parents were supposed to write down who was allowed to pick us up if they couldn't get to the school. Worried, I said, "Why wouldn't you be able to come to school?" My mother snorted, then wrote on my note in her big loopy scrawl, "You shouldn't lie to little kids." She made me take that note back to school. When the principal called, the two of them had words.

Then she packed us into the Chevy, and took us to see the missile silos ringing Tucson. "If a nuclear bomb hits, we'll all die together," she told us. Hardly reassuring. But I never suffered the delusion that nuclear war might create an inconvenience.

The Gift

One day in fourth grade, my friend Danny brought me a necklace with a cross on it. I had never seen a necklace like this. The cross had a man on it. He looked like he was in trouble. I didn't want to wear the necklace, but I didn't want to hurt Danny's feelings, so I put it on.

Mrs. Kephart, my second grade teacher a couple of years back, came stomping up to me. I was afraid. This is the woman who yelled at a classroom of kids, "Line up at the bubblah!" We looked at each other. She got furious. Nobody knew what she was talking about. She berated us for not knowing that "bubbler" was the proper term for "drinking fountain." Another day, I couldn't get the two parts of my jacket's zipper to match up. Mrs. Kephart announced to the class, "Maybe Peggy should be in kindergarten."

So I didn't want her to have anything to say to me now.

"*You* aren't Catholic, *are* you?" she snarled.

"No," I said.

"Then come with me." She grabbed my wrist and stormed up to the principal's office.

Mrs. Vernon looked down over her enormous breasts, Mount Vernon staring down at me. She dangled the necklace in her hand. "Where did you get this?"

I didn't want to get my friend in trouble. He was a good boy. "I don't know," I said.

Mrs. Kephart fumed. "We should call her mother."

"Just a minute," Mount Vernon said. "You need to tell us where this came from. You didn't steal it, did you?"

"No," I said, "It was a gift."

"From . . . ?" She lifted her eyebrows, and I knew she wouldn't give up till she found out.

I had never been in the principal's office except to bring a message or to receive an award. This was too much for me. "Danny Hernandez," I said.

"Thank you." The beads rattled onto the top of her desk. "You can go back to class now."

The hall monitor came into our room, called Danny's name, and took him down the corridor, toward Mrs. Vernon's office.

What exactly had we done wrong?

I figured that the necklace had something to do with church, but what?

When Danny came back, he kept his eyes to himself.

Later, Mrs. Garner told me how some people use the beads on that kind of necklace to pray, and people who don't use necklaces to pray aren't supposed to have them.

I don't know if Danny fessed up to taking the rosary from his mom. I don't know if he just wanted me to have one because it was pretty, or so my soul wouldn't burn in Protestant Hell.

Why was it so hard to let children in on the rules of religion?

And why, in high school, when I finally after weeks got up my nerve to ask Randy Lewis to an MYF hayride, did his mother come on the phone and say, "My son can't go to any non-Catholic activities."

I wanted to hold his hand, not sing him hymns. Which was probably worse.

Rolling River

Miss Ervin was the artsy fifth grade teacher, the one who strummed her dulcimer between arithmetic and social studies while we sang "Oh Shenandoah, I love your daughter." I had no clue who Shenandoah was or what his daughter might look like, but I loved the line "A-a-way, you rolling river." I tried to picture a river wide enough to roll, a river with water in it all the time, not like the arroyos around here, dry except for a trickle or flood once a year.

Mrs. Burnham was the tough fifth grade teacher. She wasn't amused when Gary Givens connected the dots of his freckles to draw a blue ballpoint picture of Huckleberry Hound. She made him scrub his skin with rough brown paper towels and gritty pink soap that fell when we pressed up on the lever.

Above all else, Mrs. Burnham valued hard work, so mostly we worked hard. She was absolutely consistent, which I appreciated. We knew we would not get an A for an 89. But we also knew where everything was in her classroom, including each of us. When my family was coming apart, it was a comfort to know that if something bad happened to me, Mrs. Burnham would notice.

From her set jaw, we came to understand that learning was something that would benefit us later. What a shock then one day in November when she was late. She was never late. This day, though, no teacher blew her whistle on time to call us back in from the playground. The teachers came out in a hushed bunch from the multi-purpose room, gathered us without speaking. Mrs. Burnham's face was rearranged. If she didn't hold it just right, it might break into a million pieces and scatter under the desks. We sat down, even the boys.

Mrs. Burnham passed out construction paper, the big sheets.

She told us, "We're going to take the rest of the afternoon to think, boys and girls. Let's think about what our country means to us. Let's think about . . ." Then a color I'd never seen took over her face. She went to her desk, fumbled for the chair, and put her face on the blotter. Her back, her shoulders, jerked. The more she tried not to, the harder she cried. When she could lift her face, she looked out at us. She looked far, as if we were in the foreground and she wanted to survey the whole land. I knew right then that our world had changed, but how?

"I have something to tell you," she said, swallowing. "President Kennedy has been shot."

Kids looked around as much as they could without moving. We looked around as if we were in trouble, blamed.

After school, boys ran to the arroyo, then shot each other with mesquite sticks. Those idiots took a ridiculously long time to die.

At home, Mom crunched aluminum foil onto each of the rabbit ears. Even Walter Cronkite looked shaky. Over and over a convertible rolled down a street. Then guys riding the bumper jumped into the back seat. Over and over, the pictures of Jackie, her clothes all bloodied.

I imagined the doctors up to their elbows trying to put the President's head back together. We all hoped. We hoped the way you hope Romeo and Juliet won't really die, even though Shakespeare tells you from the get-go they will.

I imagined everything leaking out, everything he had learned, everything he dreamed, all his secrets.

Hours paced around. Walter Cronkite's voice: "President Kennedy is dead."

For the next four days, nobody went to school, nobody went to work, nobody left the grainy Philco. We watched a parade, immaculate horses, then one horse with no rider, the boots backwards in the stirrups. A little boy saluted, little boy in short pants. Wasn't he cold? Why didn't anybody snuggle him? And his sister, on display, in shock. No hugs. Their mother was scary, draped in black, her grief. That veil, nearly sheer, no privacy.

Poor Kids

We didn't just have a box for the poor kids. My mom took us in our battered pushbutton Studebaker to Meyers Street, where whole families lived in railroad cars. She took us when it was hot, crayon-melting hot, out behind cotton fields where migrant workers lived in shelters they made themselves. Patchwork of cardboard, plywood, plastic, cloth. We brought what we'd collected. We offered what we could. Not enough.

My college friend Evelia lived a few weeks at a time in camps like those. She picked up pecans after machines shook the trees. She taught herself English. She stood on round rungs all day long and snapped oranges off their stems. She bent down for strawberries and lettuce, reached under the vines for grapes, stretched far and wide for plums and peaches. Her whole family beside her, she picked long sacks of cotton. Her hands bled from the bolls. She taught herself to read. Exquisite privacy, her two languages silent on pages, unless she gave voice to the words.

Good Times

Once we took a vacation. We drove to California, went to see killer whales in too-small tanks splashing families just like ours, paddled canoes in brown water, felt our rocket shake as it took off for Tomorrowland. We stopped in Vegas on the way home. My mom forgot two pillows at the motel and insisted that we drive back for them. They were in the special pillowcases, the ones with tatting around the mouths. Dad grumbled, but he drove back.

When we got home, our friends yelled, "What'd ya do?" "We got to sleep in a tent!" we yelled back.

Once after a car trip long enough to put us to sleep, we played possum. Both parents recognized we were pretending, limp in our dreams, just so we'd be carried into the house. Neither one slapped our legs, said, "Get up, you fakers. Walk." Instead, they scooped us up, propped us warm on their shoulders and bumped shut the car doors gently with their hips.

Once in Tucson it snowed. Dad took home movies while Mom tried to teach us to make a snowman. We wore socks on our hands. They got wet pretty fast. Then we wanted to go inside. Our boxer dog tried to walk six inches off the ground. The last frames show Mom throwing snowballs into the arroyo. Then at the movie camera.

Once at a Musician's Union barbecue, the piñata broke just as it hit the perfect spot in its arc. Candy showered us.

Once we took to Himmel Park tomato sandwiches with Miracle Whip on Wonder bread. No bruises on the pears. Plenty of ice in the chest. Dad pushed us on the swings. Mom tossed her hair, golden corona of soft curls backlit in the sun. They smiled at each other, smiled as if they knew something nobody else knew. Nobody that day wanted to be anywhere else. Nobody that day wanted to be anybody else. Nobody that day cried. Dad pushed us higher than we'd ever gone before, higher than the bar that held the bolts that held the chains we clutched so hard. Dad pushed us. Top of the arc—held there in midair, suspended, the chains widening, that thump scary heartbeat, then the thrill backwards falling, legs bent, face down, facing the shallow graves scraped under each swing, then rising back, lifting taller even than our father reaching his huge warm gentle hand to swoop us forward, down and amazingly up again.

Breakup

Is this how the river feels? To us, the river changes slowly, taking whole seasons to freeze or thaw. But maybe for the river it feels quick, reckless. Breakup, the ultimate hot flash. The river outside my window, frozen and thawed every year since it was a river.

Just days before the first Canada geese arrive, the last few skiers risk their lives on the river, a runner takes a last few laps on ice, a dog stops to bite mushy snow.

One day dark leads reveal where the ice is rotten. Overflow bubbles up, refreezes. The leads widen every afternoon. We wake before daylight when geese gather to take a look, mosey over the ice shores, then drop into frigid water for a swim.

In geological time, this isn't even a blink.

Two days later, swans, where we don't expect them. Tundra swans twine necks among snowflakes vanishing into evening's river. Past break up, tablecloths of rotten ice nest along the bank. Halfway, swan wings open, then settle in like second thoughts.

Maybe they flew north over Minto, traced halos over brooding ponds, saw from far up without touching the world is hard and will stay hard a while longer.

∽

I think I am mending. I have been home from the hospital three days, sleeping mostly, after the exhaustion of care so intensive I couldn't rest. Mitch has flown up from Washington to help us, and brought Nathan, age two, and his great good energy.

"How you are doing, Peggy?" he smiles. We have just finished our lunch of halibut corn chowder, and Nathan runs to get a

87

yogurt pop, brings it for me to open. I rip the wrapper, and that fast can't get air.

Can't. Get. Air.

I can feel breath going into my body, but it isn't getting where it needs to go. I pull in more air, faster. I find a way to call out. Dizzy. Working harder than I've ever worked. I begin to float above my body. Mitch reassures Nathan. Nobody cries.

Joe calls my surgeon who tells us to get to the hospital, don't wait for an ambulance. They somehow lift me into the wheelchair. I remember Nathan's asking, "Where we are going?" From the back seat, Mitch holds my head up, talks to me, pats my face.

∞

The first attendant at Fairbanks Memorial nails it. "You have all the signs of pulmonary embolism. Usually we'd give you clot-busters, but let's see. Nope. You're not a candidate—head trauma *and* recent surgery. Too risky." They take me for x-rays so they can see exactly what they're dealing with.

The technician lines me up just right inside a machine that will move full circle around my chest. "Ok, relax. Just breathe normally," she advises. *If I could do that I wouldn't be here*, I think. I don't have air to say anything. The films show a saddle embolism blocking both lungs, massive. By now no one can find a pulse. I'm so tired.

They discuss a ventilator. They discuss a dose of tPA, which might make me bleed in the hurt places in my body, in my brain. They discuss putting me on a medevac plane to Anchorage where a thoracic surgeon could possibly open me to remove the clot.

What we don't know is that the surgical procedure to remove a pulmonary embolism has never been performed successfully in Alaska, and rarely anywhere else.

What I do know is that I will die if I go in that plane. I tell them I want the drugs that might break up the clot. Joe agrees.

I tell Joe my love. I whisper messages for him to tell my family. Just before they insert the ventilator tube down my throat, I mouth what could be my last spoken words.

The guy numbs what needs numbing. I do not remember fighting him. He gives me another dose so I can't resist, and plumbs my airway. It's a new kind of helplessness, to be without a voice. With the machine breathing for me, I slip in and out of awareness.

Dr. Arva Chiu, a courageous young internist, administers the risky drug. In a few hours, we'll know. I doze.

∞

Lungs saddled up for the embolus express, I am the nightmare. Who is my rider? Of all those who've gone before could it be the one I most long to see?

Or, packhorse overloaded, am I lugging heavy as slump blocks strapped to my chest all the children I never nursed?

Spurring me down the stretch, let it be you, you my love, and gravid curiosity.

∞

Before the tube choked off words, I spoke. To my husband I said what might be the last. I barely understood what they intended, only that they wanted desperately to help. After the first numbing, I fought. After the second, my resisting, instinctive, was no match for their gentleness. For forty-five minutes an aide squeezed plastic bulb-fuls of air into my lungs. Weeks later, reading dictated notes, I find out a machine breathed for me for two days.

Where are they, those days? Where are those days that slip away as surely as breath?

∞

Ever notice that when you get that advice, "Just breathe normally," you can never do it?

When you're handed a six-foot rosy boa, when a tarantula

tangles his arm's hair in yours, when you sneak up with a Dixie cup to catch a scorpion, when you're maintaining in front of your friend's parents, when before surgery you're counting backwards from one hundred, when for the first time you fit a snorkel between your teeth and put your mask into water, when the dog they said doesn't bite clearly intends to, when you tell that necessary lie, when your scuba instructor tells you to take the giant stride into two hundred feet of ocean, when they slide you tight into the MRI tube, when you stand to give your speech, when yellow cups of oxygen fall from the plane's ceiling, when the respiratory therapist clips together your nostrils, when the dentist packs your mouth with cotton logs, when you get the news you've been waiting for, when you get the news you've been dreading, when you stand up before God and everybody to pledge your love to your mate, just breathe normally.

∞

My friend Frank calls his med tech brother, Moose, to ask about pulmonary embolism. Moose's first question, "Is your friend alive?"

∞

I wish I could tell you that a near-death experience makes a person wiser or more profound, more compassionate or generous. It does slow a person down, in good ways as well as bad.

It's not so bad to lie still on clean sheets and savor the first thing you see each time you wake up. In the morning, yes, and then all through the day, breathing slowly to bring the room into focus.

∞

Weeks later, reading my medical charts with the sordid thrill of a voyeur, I say, "Joe, they got this wrong, didn't they? It says I was on the ventilator two days. Wasn't it about forty-five minutes?" Joe looks at me as if I've just arrived on the planet.

"It *was* two days. The guy used the ambu bag to squeeze air in by hand for forty-five minutes." I take this in.

∽

During those long hours, what does Joe do?

How do you spend what may be the last hours you have with your beloved when the beloved is unaware?

∽

Next door to me in intensive care, they bring in a young woman who has survived a head-on crash that killed six other people. She's completely cut loose from this earth—doesn't know who or where she is, doesn't know what year it is. The nurse keeps reminding her that her mother's on the way. But the mom's coming up from Utah, so the daughter's in limbo for now. She cannot identify the parts of her own body. They've told her that she's eighteen. They've not yet told her she's a widow.

I cannot see. I cannot see her, but I can hear.

∽

The voice yelling in the wilderness doesn't know what year it is, doesn't know how old it is, doesn't know its own name.

The voice pleading in the wilderness can't recall how it got here, doesn't know where this is, can't locate its hands.

The voice echoing in the wilderness can't guess how many fingers or why, no matter how intensive the care, doesn't know it's married to silence.

∽

Hurt, lost, bereft, cut loose, searching. Wild inside and out, each of us who breathes.

∽

What I took for granted: whole hours without pain. Turning my head. Sending a hand the signal to lift from the bed and having it do so without complaint. Having both eyes following the same choreographer.

∽

I think of how differently Joe has suffered, how different this feels to him. He tells me that every thirty minutes they used a long needle to draw arterial blood from deep in my inner thigh. I don't remember that at all. He tells me that Mitch put Nathan to sleep on a sofa in the waiting area, and kept calling my family and Joe's family with updates. Joe tells me that with each of his six kids, he's been terrified at one time or another. But he thinks this whole episode has made him the most scared he's ever been.

He tries to remind me—"In intensive care, on the ventilator, you were so thirsty, remember?" And then I do. ICE COLD LEMON-ADE I scrawled on the yellow pad. Joe picked up a little lollipop of a swab and moistened my lips and tongue. The mechanism down my throat would have sent liquid straight into the lungs, for sure. I bit down so hard once, Joe said, I damn near snapped the stick in half. I remember thirst.

I try to imagine Joe, massively bruised, waiting with me. He kept glancing at my blood oxygen level, and knew it didn't look good.

In my chart, a doctor I can't recall writes, "Pale woman on stretcher. Patient is in extremis." I wonder if this is the second worst thing someone can write, next to "Time of death." And I guess that depends upon whether you wish to keep living or not.

I celebrate his error.

∽

What makes me bite down hard and not let go? It's animal, ferocious, how I want this life.

∽

The intern breaks a tongue depressor to make a point. He has a Q-tip in the other hand. He touches me at every critical juncture, and my only job is to say *sharp, sharp, dull, sharp, dull dull dull.*

∞

I gain a reputation as a "hard stick." Every sharp inquiry comes up dry. Blood turns shy. Arteries shut so far down doctors can't touch a pulse. They hold their breath, listen. Again. As if it suspects it doesn't contain infinite secrets (or any, lately) the body holds on to what it can.

∞

Neck crimped, I have no strength to push against the mat of my own hair. We call our haircutter, who comes to the hospital. Cheery as usual, Penny says, "I can comb this out." My hair used to reach down to the center of my back. Now it's a wad of road kill about the size of a mashed cat.

"No thanks," I tell her. I couldn't bear the tugging, don't have any energy for vanity.

Shorn, I dream I can levitate.

∞

When you have traveled to the edge, looked over, pulled back, when a machine has drawn breath for you for a day, for two, when your bruises, travel stickers for trips you don't remember, haven't faded, but you've come back, back to some sense of self, what do you want?

First, a shower. You cannot believe the stench near death, how it clings. But you have to get a special dispensation, and help. The doc says all right, just not too hot. It's slow, leaning down the hallway on Joe, the IV stand tangling. The shower has thank God a chair, but no hand-held head. Superhuman strength this will take. No. Just more than you've got.

Aiming the body toward water, you take no breath for granted. Aiming toward water the body. Aiming toward cleansing, toward breath.

∽

One MRI technician is kind, and keeps talking to me all through the procedure. The second time, though, I get a man whose significant other is this machine. He speaks to it, but doesn't answer me. His tattoos, carpeting both arms, scare me. He looks like the kind of guy who nails stuffed animals to trees.

I'm surrounded, in too small a space. Noise bombards every cell. I close my good eye, recite song lyrics, hymns, every poem I know. The machine hammers all around me.

I keep coming back to Neruda's socks, rabbit soft, knit of twilight and goatskin, his feet morphing into blackbirds, cannons, sharks, decrepit firemen. The only way I make it through those two hours is thinking of myself as a fugitive, reminding myself that

> beauty is twice
> beauty
> and what is good is doubly
> good
> when it is a matter of two socks
> made of wool
> in winter.

My toes turn to ice. Finally I have to yell. The guy doesn't answer. Does not answer. I yell again. Long pause, eerie. Did I make sound? He slides me out of the huge machine like a loaf on a baker's peel. "Okay, I'm through with you." He walks away. His assistant apologizes, helps me sit up.

∽

The first food to nourish my broken body slides in through the IV, invisible. Next comes the "clear liquid diet," transpar-

94

ent nourishment to see me through. The tray arrives. This meal was clearly designed by a second grade class: popsicle, red Jell-O, cran-grape juice box, sugared tea, a handful of Jolly Rancher candies. And because there's always someone responsible in second grade, a cup of broth.

∞

The nurses, attentive, calm, brave, admit they were scared, too. Some I was too groggy to remember, but I remember the kind one who was hugely pregnant, how I felt guilty each time I made her walk. Her swollen ankles. And the quick slender one with glasses who stayed with me when panic lurched into my throat. And the ones who cleaned me, cleaned up after me, the ones who wiped my body when I could not. At first, I was embarrassed, deeply. Then I watched them, watched carefully the dignity of their work wiping away the indignities of injury.

∞

One nurse notices the pattern of inch-wide polka dots across my lower abdomen. Is this from medication? Yes, from Combi-patch hormone replacement therapy, stuck on since doctors removed my uterus and ovaries last year. She's horrified, sure that estrogen is contraindicated. This could cause more strokes. We tear off the current patch, leaving a red circle, raw as just-plowed ground.

My friend Susan calls hers "power surges." Another friend muses that in Alaska in winter, hot flashes could be attractive in a bedmate. All I know is my body's minding its own business. Then one blink and every pore opens. I'm flushed, racing, slick. Radiating, but hardly radiant. The sheets cling, sodden. Joe's hands, soothing as riverbanks, cool me.

∞

Where are they, those days? Where are those days that slip away as surely as breath?

oso

When my grandmother lived in an old folks' home, there were three buildings—one for people who could still get around pretty well, one for people who needed help with bathing and dressing and walking, and one for those who needed full-time nursing care. Grandma said, "Nobody wants to go to the East Building. Nobody gets out of there alive."

Like everybody else, I want out of the East Building.

oso

In my dream Canadians are trying to save the dwindling Chisana woodland herd of caribou. Predators ravage the few that remain, so rangers and volunteers construct an enormous corral around several acres. Every gravid female they can find they herd inside. Rangers keep them there until they drop their calves. When the calves are more than ten days old, they have a fighting chance to evade wolves and bears. So the corral gates will open then.

Inside the corral of my hospital bed, I dream a whorl of caribou, stamping a great spiral in the snow.

THREE

Constants

My grandma tells me, "You were always an odd combination of old lady and little girl." She also says, "I don't think people change all that much in their lives."

Maybe not. But I feel changed, once I know how to read. I spend hours every day in a world of my own. Large daily doses of other people's lives I take in like breath. Other people's houses—so not everyone lives like we do. Good. Large doses of other people's suffering—no, no, don't let that happen, no, no don't let them hurt. But they do. How do we live with that? Large doses of other people's celebrations, their joys my own secret joys. How to find my way around. How to negotiate. How to say, "That is yours. This is mine. This is ours." The nature of so many loves, never simple, the nature of possibility. This I learn from reading.

Mr. and Mrs. Earl Penny

My dad's boss, Earl Penny, was coming for dinner. Mr. and Mrs. Penny, in our house. We carted out the mountain of newspapers on the round coffee table. We cleaned everything, dusted every curl of wrought iron on the room divider. Mom spent weeks on the menu, days on the cooking. We got new clothes.

At the last minute, Mom looked at the sectional couch and decided to wash the cushion covers, just so everything would be perfect. We unzipped zippers we were never allowed to touch, and threw the heavy fabric in the washer. Then we hung them out to dry.

A couple of hours before the Pennys were supposed to get there, Mom, her hair tight in pincurls, tried to stuff the first foam back into its sheath. Not happening. Somehow the foam had grown. We compressed each cushion as hard as we could, but it ballooned out of every crack between our fingers.

Mom retreated into her bedroom, her face a mess. I talked her into the shower, into putting on the dress she'd made, a peasant look with a tight fitted midriff and a poofy white part offering her breasts.

When the doorbell rang, though, she could hardly make a sentence. I invited the Pennys in, had them sit on chairs from the dinette set. Still trying to jam a wayward corner into cloth, I told them how we had washed these, just for them. Mrs. Penny grimaced down at me, her hair shellacked, beauty-parlor stiff. She made a chilly attempt at politeness. Mr. Penny obviously didn't think it was his place to talk to children.

My mother brought in drinks in tall glasses I'd never seen her use. Ice cubes clinked.

It's odd. I don't remember my dad being there at all.

∾

Dad sold the first Addressograph-Multigraph machines in Tucson, a new territory for the company. He sold forty-seven the first year and everybody was happy. He hired my uncle Dan as his assistant salesman. Then a new boss, Mr. Penny, came into the office. He'd make promises about what the machines could do, and customers would say, "We need to check with John to make sure that'll work." Mr. Penny couldn't stand that.

Dad and Dan had just made the biggest sale of their lives, a $22,000 order. They stopped in at a pub for lunch, and stayed to shoot a game of pool. Somehow Mr. Penny found out where they were. He came blasting into the bar and bellowed, "So this is what you do when I'm out of town!" He told Dad he could either transfer to another office or quit. Betrayed and angry, Dad quit.

Mr. Penny pocketed the commission.

Scorpions

We spent cool November hunting scorpions in the Rincons, turning rocks with our sneaker toes, checking with twisted-off greasewood switches first the darker upturned faces of stone, then the sandy rock shallows. We whisked fuzzy seedpods over the moistness, hunting the striped or tan little hook of poison curled over. We'd scoop them up in Dixie cups and walk them level back to camp, back to the circle of rock we'd set hemming in paper plates and dry mesquite that gave us back our fingers chilled to curls. The scorpions would scramble against steep daffodils waxing the sides of the cup, so we'd calm them with a glug or two of beer. Once Gin floated hers, damn near got stung before it drowned. Mostly, we squished the soppy cup between two firepit rocks and watched. Most of the beer left in a huff. The scorpion caught a clawhold on the seam and clambered up. For a moment it wavered, twitching. Then the edge of the cup clenched in on itself, petals pressing back to the bulb, the trapped one ticking inside.

Picking Bricks

Tucson summer picking bricks, two for a nickel, tossing chips and cracks, we rip fingers out of cheap garden gloves, out of oven mitts two sizes too big. We pick brickyard seconds hot as the comal where test drops skitter, our sweat drops big as pop beads. We're drips picking bricks with Mr. Watson, twisted-legs mean, who swats the closest kid with his crutch to hurry us up, Mr. Watson whose leg braces sear bare skin.

Picking bricks we're glad we ate sugar cubes so we won't get what he has, whatever twists inside him sweat slick. Hands harden into brick-holds, culls tossed, gleaners lining the scrap-wood trailer. Then home, where patio sand level and tamped rests damp in cool shade.

We set brick edge up, basket weave, slant border, carting brick till we limp, till Mrs. Watson offers sun tea with ice, oasis in our palms.

Thunderclouds lift the sun, that anvil, off our backs. Rubber mallets pound level red patterns burnished with us, floating bubbles, brick dust.

Landfraud Nosebleed

In Sonoran desert around Tucson, some developments rose up fast as bad dreams, each house the same as every other one on the block. Other places carpetbaggers made promises, made people see their dreams. They sold lots, sold the same lots over and over, then disappeared.

For entertainment, for free food, my folks took us. They listened to the spiels, but never bought a thing. They scammed the scam artists there in the desert. I thought about the land, about the people who came before us, about people who stayed.

We'd be out in the desert fifteen miles from Fort Huachuca checking out the latest bogus development—street signs tilting in caliche, no water, no electricity, just salesmen yapping like freshly groomed poodles and my strapped parents nodding, nodding but never talking, never signing, just polite till the Mexican cooks opened the pit and FREE BBQ smoke watered our eyes and mouths.

Right then, on cue, my mother would glance over just as my nose flooded, blots big as summer raindrops staining my crop top and shorts, and the salesman running up with a Dixie cup of crushed ice, almost heaven if I didn't hold it too long to the bridge of my nose . . .

Then plates of shredded beef and pinto beans, green chilies and white bread appeared like mirages—plenty, enough, too much, so we ate what we could, said thanks, really, foiled the rest and balanced paper plates on bare knees all the way, tissues mashed to my tilted-back face, getting away with it, all the way home.

Saguaros tied up in surveyor's tape, cacti packing heat, held their own seeds hostage on high, Apache tears packed buckshot tight. The cracker box trailer-office got hauled off to the next patch of creosote and jumping cactus. The dirt stayed. Trash hung around, blew off with dust devils, snagged on barb wire. Before the heat of the day, uprooted Yaqui women whose third language tasted metallic, sharp blades of English on the tongue, rose, lifted saguaro ribs and ocotillo spikes to whap down fruit out of reach. They picked up those strong enough not to split, left behind those broken, bleeding into a new generation.

Canteens

Almost all the desert that formed my imagination is now under buildings. Now very few kids will lug half-gallon canteens into desert. Very few kids will come alive in an open place so vast they could imagine the first people who walked there. Very few kids will have enough desert to imagine how this place would look without people in it.

Maybe now parents don't let their kids wander from breakfast till sundown, knowing if anything awful happened, somebody would run home and tell.

Shoes

In junior high, my accomplice David Bromberg approached an unsuspecting kid on the playground.

"Go ask Peggy what size shoes her father wears," he suggested. The kid, puzzled, sidled up to me.

"What size shoes does your father wear?"

I put my face down, glanced out through downcast lashes.

"That's not funny. My father got his legs shot off in the war." Horrified, the kid would turn to David. One offered to hammer him into the ground. Another cried. Another said, disgusted, "That's not true. I know your dad."

We played that scene over and over until too many kids knew and nobody would fall for it. We never laughed. We just watched, hard, to see what would happen.

The Draft

"You have pubic hair, so you have to know this," my mother says. Her eyes glint, hard and sharp as shards of thrown bottles. She's holding toward me a brown bottle, liquid prescribed for her, and a handful of cotton.

"What?" I say.

"Crabs. Your father brought them home to us. *Lice.*" Her face twists as if the word itself tastes horrible. I am ashamed to look at her. "Check your panties for little dots of blood. That's how you can tell. And wash all your underwear in pure hot water." She's in great pain. She's also reveling in revealing all this, in shoving all this on me. "If you itch down there, use cotton to dab on this stuff." It's a new mother's milk, this fluid held out to me by an earthbound fury.

How much does she wish to spare me the disgrace of clawing at my coiled hairs? How much does she need to avoid having nits reinfect the whole household? How much does she wish to enlist me in her suffering, in her war, to conscript me as witness, conspirator, spy? How much does she want to add my anger to hers, backdraft already burning all the oxygen?

Their passion for one another must have been very fierce for her anger to be this strong. *Don't try to make me hate him. Don't make me hate you*, I think. I'm disgusted with both of them.

She wants me to know exactly who I'm dealing with. I do, not entirely in the ways she intends.

I misread the label, "Apply generosity."

Western

For Rodeo Week in February, girls got to wear jeans to school. Even if we couldn't afford to go see the bucking broncs and Brahma bulls and barrel riders, we got to wear western clothes to school. Shirts with snaps at the cuffs, shirts stitched with ruffles or with big V shapes across the shoulders. Stetsons if you were rich, straw hats if you were regular. This was a big deal.

Any other week, girls had to wear dresses, and not too short. The test was, if Mrs. Cox made you kneel, your dress better touch the asbestos tiles on the hallway floor. (And boys whose hair touched their shirt collars had to go home until it was trimmed.)

Understand that I was not a troublemaker. I studied. I got good grades. I insisted that my siblings go to school.

The first day of Rodeo Week I didn't have any jeans. I substituted a pair of bell bottoms, hot pink hip huggers I made myself. Cowboys have bell bottoms, I knew, to pull over the fancy stitching on their boots. I got the kids ready, and ran to school.

My first period teacher sent me to the dean of girls. Mrs. Cox said my outfit wasn't western enough. I would have to go home and change. I cried all the way, angry and hurt. I failed every class I missed that day, no make-ups.

I didn't have the props, the costume. I didn't have anything. What could I change into?

Rodeo Clowns

Imagine the thrill of distracting the bull so the fallen rider can
push up out of sawdust and manure and leap the arena fence.

Funny thing—even a winning ride lasts only eight seconds.

Then there's another sharp set of horns attached to a ton of
kicking, twisting, pestered and pissed Brahma bull.

Ragbag

Dad never hid his beer, except from his own parents. Mom, though, couldn't admit why her "naps" never left her rested. At first, I wondered *Does every family have a rag bag? Does every family have vodka bottles stashed in their rag bag?* Even if it was important, we weren't supposed to interrupt her buzz. She had a temper and a mouth. Alcohol amplified both. Before long we realized that we weren't supposed to notice, weren't supposed to mention what she denied. She swaddled her secrets, her self, in our stained and torn and worn through garments.

Wail

After school I threw in a load of wash, cleaned up the bathroom, and sliced open a package of hot dogs for dinner. I arranged the wieners on the broiler pan, popped them in the oven, and piled the clothes on my arms to hang out.

I was about halfway through pinning shirttail to shirttail when Mom came roaring out with a stick from the broom closet. She grabbed my arm and wailed on me, hard.

"What's the matter with you?" I yelled.

"You could have burnt the house down," she screamed, still hitting me.

"Okay, stop! Stop! Sorry. Jeez." I glared at her. Then I had to pick wet clothes out of the dirt and start all over.

Getting Ready

When my younger sister Sue asks me about sex, I think *This is Mom's job*. Then I think again. She did a so-so job with me, showing me The Book, making sure I saw the facts-of-life film at school—a pink cartoon that told us not to worry about blood on our panties. The voiceover advised cheerfully, "Just have a Kotex pad and belt ready!"

Then one day Mom called me into the bathroom. Each pin-curl severe inside its boundary of scalp, parted off by the rattail, anchored with a cross, she called me in to answer questions I hadn't asked. She toweled her calves. Her breasts flopped like rag dolls toward her waist when she stood. One foot on the toilet seat, she reached down there. Her tug delivered the mouse inside her, clot-covered slime nestling in toilet paper so I won't be afraid when it happens to me.

∞

The parents were still married back then. For Sue, though, life is different. Mom is fiercer, harder to read, hardly ever there. I think, *Maybe this will remind Mom that we need her. Maybe this will bring her back, at least a little. Maybe.* I have this irrational hope.

I say, "Mom should tell you about this."

"Uh uh. No. Noooo," Sue groans. Her eyes are big.

"Come on," I insist. I drag her toward the back bathroom where Mom's getting ready for a date. Sue's thrashing out of my grip, pulling back, hiding behind me.

Just out of the shower, Mom unwinds the towel around her hair, pats herself dry. She picks up the little square glass bottle of Avon Perfumed Deodorant, shakes a puddle in the palm of one hand, then splashes the opposite underarm. She steps in, one foot at a time, then bends to grasp the edges of her girdle. Her breasts, pendulous as any in the *Geographic*, flap around as she yanks up her rubber casing an inch at a time. Yank, flop, yank, flop. Sweat makes the girdle stick, resist. Her bra she fastens in front, then turns the hooks to the back, slips her arms through the straps. She cups both breasts like weapons she's aiming.

"WHAT?" she yells.

"Sue has something important to ask you," I counter.

"WELL, WHAT?" She turns her glare to Sue, who's trying hard to be invisible. On the rims of both eyes water gathers. So still, Sue won't let one drop spill, not in front of Mom.

"Never mind." I take Sue into our room, put my arms around her, murmur to soothe her, offer her what little I know.

∞

When sobs broke out of us and we stood shaking with childhood's sorrows, my mother had a solution. She yelled. She yelled, "You want something to cry about? Huh?" With her red face close to ours, she thundered, "I'll give you something to cry about." If we could, we shut up. She made us shut up tight as gunpowder tamped into a blast hole, the fuse sticking out like a tongue.

Rights, Pictures

Life magazine showed up every week. My dad said that was one reason he quit the safe job his dad got him as a letter carrier. He just couldn't bear every blasted week to be weighed down by *Life*.

On the back cover, an advertiser's idea of a doctor wore on his forehead a round disk about as big as the lid of a mason jar. It had a hole in the middle. I never did find out what that was for. No doctor I ever saw had one. This doctor leaned forward so you would trust him, or if you didn't trust him, you would at least obey. People obeyed doctors in those days. You were supposed to hear the caption in his voice, the voice of Robert Young in *Father Knows Best*: "I recommend Camels for all my patients who smoke."

Dogs and fire hoses, one week. German Shepherds and open nozzles set on little kids, kids dressed up in Sunday school clothes. I was terrified that people would do such a thing. Maybe we'd be next. I knew where the closest hydrant was. I asked my mother why grown men would hurt kids like this.

"Because they're afraid," she said.

"What country is this?" I asked.

"Every country in the world," she said.

"But right now, which country is doing this right now?"

"Ours. Right now it's our country."

Homecoming

The year my uncle Jack came back from Vietnam I remember as unbearably hot. We swiped chunks of two-by-fours heaped by cracking slabs poured for houses exactly like ours, set the wood on melting asphalt so our kickstands would hold. Otherwise, they sank in, left pedals digging their own graves right where they fell.

The developer shaved off all the desert plants and planted tract homes. We still found a few survivors—horny toads in shady corners, kangaroo rats in the dog chow.

We made a banner—Welcome Home Jack—and draped it across the garage door at my uncle Dan's house. The first night Jack got in, we grilled steaks from American Meat Company and made a big salad. (I peeled the cucumbers, careful to rub the cut end in a circle three times to draw out the bitterness.)

When I first saw Jack, I held back. His eyes let me know that a hug was all right, welcome even. He looked skinny, tired, maybe sick. Mom had warned us not to ask about the war, not to congratulate him on his medals, not to mention his wife and child. Fay, his rich, spoiled teenaged British bride, had languished in Mountain Home, Idaho, where she gave birth, then had grown bored in Sausalito where they had set up house. She packed up their infant son and returned to her father's mansion across the ocean.

All I knew was that Jack was a hero. He flew small spotter planes close to the ground and dropped smoke for the bombers to use as targets. Only years later would I begin to comprehend how that meant he could see the people there, no way to tell who was an enemy, could see the starved kids, the animals, could see whole villages of huts that would be destroyed. He could also see U.S. troops he might not be able to shield or help. He had to see what was left of many of his friends, had to imagine what was never seen again. He had to see shapes zipped into body bags.

The second night, a hot night, my mom put on a pot of her famous swiss steak. She scrubbed and poked the baked potatoes. Fresh sun tea for the kids, beer for the adults. She worked all day to get the house ready. My dad took off on a motorcycle ride just before Jack arrived. I was glad Mom and Jack had those few hours together, glad they had a private moment.

But Dad didn't come back. The table was set. We had finally just poured the tea over the ice when my dad roared up, scraping the Harley's back wheel over the straggling African daisies my mom kept shaded. He loves me, he loves me not.

"Jack!" he yelled, "Come take a look at my bike!" Jack went out to look at the '64 Sportster, cherried, candy-apple red with black trim. Dad was laughing, loud, his bar laugh. Jack told Dad dinner was on the table. Then he ducked back inside.

Dad drew in big lungs-ful of beer breath. He drew open the sliding glass door and yelled, "Hey, Honey, let's not go to any trouble. Let's go out for dinner and drinks."

He went over to the splay-legged couch where Jack was sitting, his back not touching the Naugahyde. Dad never even asked how Jack was. Instead, he started talking motorcycles.

"We have a dirt track out in the desert, want to come see?"

"Not right now." Jack could hardly look at him. I felt so sorry that Jack, just home from the war, had to see this.

Mom had that eerie calm that meant her temper was plumping up her whole body. She calmly walked into the kitchen, put on hot mitts and dumped the whole pot, sauce and steak, in the trash. Then she unjammed the junk drawer and dug around for our split-handled ball peen hammer.

Whoosh of cool air released as she scraped open the sliding door. She walked, deadly calm, over to my father's motorcycle.

Like a musician, she held the hammer head high, waited for the right breath.

Then she exhaled. On cue, she sank the rounded end with cool precision tank tank tank across the sexy paint until we could have set up Chinese checkers.

My father ran out, stared. Stared. Then he grabbed her wrists, hard enough to bruise. He grabbed her wrists and tried to force her back into the house. Jack came to the door and said, "Don't. You. Hit. Her. Don't." My mom splayed herself like a big X across the opening. They struggled, the grownups.

Pearls

After the divorce, my mother wore a single pearl on a gold chain, and a single pearl ring in a simple setting. Beauty created by irritation, irritation that demanded beauty, her last two drops. Her last ornaments, last evidence that milky orbs from the sea could set off her own beauty, she sacrificed. Bitter, that the pawnshop attendant could smell her desperation, offered twelve measly dollars. Bitter, that she left behind her pendant, her ring, and brought home Cheerios and milk, Wonder Bread, Imperial.

She drank the rest.

Pattern Pieces

One year Mom promised to make us Easter dresses. After Sue complained about having to wear the same green plaid outfit for *years*, her own, then Ginny's, then mine, handed down, Mom acquiesced, bought different colors. The same print, tulips, in pink and yellow and blue, unrolled from three different bolts. She spread the yardage on the table, smoothed it out, then pinned carefully brown tissue pattern pieces. We wanted our turns, wanted to cut out odd shapes along heavy black lines.

She held the scissors open, the cloth in their jaws. She said, "Ever wonder if, when we cut a piece of material, we're destroying whole families, neighborhoods, cities?"

Alarmed, I said, "*Are we?*"

"Who knows?" she laughed, and sliced the fabric.

&

No seams ever stitched those pieces into dresses. Mom piled them, prickly with straight pins, into the trunk in her bedroom. I'd take them out once in a while, long after even Sue had outgrown the biggest pattern.

All the things we meant to do, all the ideas we gave up on, all the possibilities that gave up on us.

Why did Mom keep them around?

&

Hanna, who cut out pattern pieces, Simplicity, along solid lines, trailing scraps of see-through tissue. Hanna, who pinned and basted, darted and smocked but hardly ever finished, bored by her own mistakes, bored by tearing out, the ripper's one snaggletooth undoing in seconds a whole day's intimate destruction. Embroidered, tailored, flat-felled seams in the fitted garment of her intelligence—unmended, splurged on checked gingham, rickrack, the tiers of a square dance skirt swing your neighbor that would sail straight out, levitate over six petticoats showing off gams too gorgeous to be wasted. Hanna, who chose turquoise checks with white arrowheads for Johnny's matching shirt, sleeves for once long enough, pearl snaps winking, flirting, each stitch an attempt to keep home his wildness, hers, this handmade shirt a cover for all he could never in words get off his chest—only to have him refuse it. Hanna, who savored above all the crossed star when women left their men waiting, and touched together their sewn-up hands to create the center of the world, turning.

∞

She kept the turquoise checked gingham cowboy shirt she made for my father, shirt that matched her homemade square dance outfit, skirt so wide it flew straight out when she twirled.

His shirt was a work of art—pearl snap buttons, white arrowheads pointing both directions at the edges of his pockets, tall snapped cuffs. He tried it on, once. He had to find a reason not to wear it, and told her finally, "A full pack of Marlboros won't fit in that pocket." He then dismissed square dancing, her one link with the adult world. He fell back on a phrase his Nazarene parents used, "Dancing's a vertical expression of a horizontal intention." (He never set foot in church, and he rejected everything his parents taught him, but there you go.) They had loud arguments about how Chuck Parker looked at Mom, loud arguments about how Dad looked at Janet Sopher. He arranged to be at jam sessions every square dance night, and she couldn't show up without a partner. Then she asked if she could come along to his dance job once in a while. He played bass at the Beachcomber, a small neighborhood bar whose owner liked live music. I'm sure she cramped his style. He'd be up on the bandstand jutting his chin to the beat, winking toward the back table at the blonde with the French twist.

Long after he left, after he married Crazy Marcia, that shirt stayed in Mom's hump-backed trunk.

∽

Sue is adamant.

"Of course she kept that stuff. That crap was her evidence. It proved she was a victim. *Oh, feel sorry for me* . . . Look, she CHOSE to be the way she was. She invited those men home. She drank. She smoked. She hit us."

I try to make the case that perhaps some things were beyond her control.

"She abused you too, in an insidious way. She made you do her job. You had to be the parent, even to her."

∽

In infants, they call it "failure to thrive." When nobody touches or holds or caresses her, when nobody listens for her, listens to her. When nobody laughs if she makes a joke, nobody picks her up if she falls. Nobody looks forward to sharing her day, nobody curls next to her at night. When nobody notices how she hurts, how she hurts herself, when nobody's strong enough to stop her. When she pushes away those who love her so often, so thoroughly, they stay away. When all that feeds her is her own rage. When she whips up her pain to make sure she's alive. At least it's not nothing. At least it's not nobody. It's her, hers, her pain.

∽

A Divorced Mother With Children—that's how she sees herself, in capital letters. Hanna stands beside a planter box denting an aluminum pan on the cranium of her daughter. The pansies stare, their pug faces flat, bewildered as that of Sing Ling, the crippled neighbor's commie dog who digs through vegetable bins, biting the purple onions of revenge. Adobe flakes off under the nails of the sullen girl scratching for balance. Something breaks inside her mother, something bigger than tantrums of embroidery, boil your life down to that goddammit a turquoise Naugahyde sectional sofa and these kids forever popping out like varicose don't lie to me shit-for-brains, how many times I got to tell ya—don't go right from wearing diapers to changing them.

Offspring

Ginny was so much like her, sharp and talkative, full of her own opinions. She and Mom clashed every day.

Sue was always afraid of both the parents. She kept hoping no one would notice her.

John was just trying to hold on, taking it all in, trying to keep one arm around anything that might float.

From both parents, I was learning how *not* to act, how *not* to be in the world.

Rollaway Geometry

I'm fifteen. My usual routine: crawl out of bed at 4:30, finish homework while it's quiet, throw in a load of wash, wake up the kids. Shower, brush teeth, throw on a Madras shift, tug a brush through my waist-length hair. Worry that it's too wavy (not stylish). Wake the kids again. Help them with cereal and milk, if we have any. Cut them a hunk of welfare commodity cheese if we don't. Get them washed and dressed and out the door. Run to Palo Verde, just in time for 7:00 a.m. Office Skills, where we clatter along on manual typewriters and push ourselves toward 100 words a minute in shorthand.

I'd put in a full day at school, then run home, hoping the little kids made it back all right, that the Siefarth twins didn't ambush them, that nobody's knees were bloody.

One morning, though, I stumbled out into the pre-dawn living room and cracked my shin. What the? I snapped on the hall light and saw the rollaway bed, set up crossways. There in their full glory were my mom and some guy, spooned, passed out. Naked. Mom's face was smeared, her breasts sucked purple.

The whole place smelled rank. Spilled beer, full ashtrays, sour flesh, scorched carpet.

She worked two dead-end jobs, collating multiple listings all day and waiting tables at a dive, the Rio Rita, all night. She'd bring home the best of a bad lot and sway to country music—"Make the world go away . . ." They'd guzzle cheap booze, smoke cheap cigarettes, smash themselves against one another.

Most nights, though, she had the sense to take them back into her room, to shut the door. I had to figure out how to make them disappear, how to make sure the kids didn't have to see this. I ran cold water over a washrag, patted it against her face.

"Mom? MOM?"

She shoved the cloth away. "What the?"

"It's morning. The kids will be up any minute."

"Shit." She tried turning over.

"No, you have to get up, right now."

"Says who?"

"Please." By then I was furious, crying. I couldn't help it. What did she think she was doing? Why didn't she even try to watch out for us?

I didn't know who this loser was, couldn't even guess how he was going to hurt her. Or maybe he was just a 200-pound balsa wood airplane, a flimsy toy she'd fly once and then crash, splintering.

"Shake me again, you're on restriction," she slurred.

Like you're ever around to enforce it, I thought. My mind flashed to the test today, midterm in geometry, tried to remember how to use what's given to do proofs.

"Now. Get up." My voice was the voice I used on kids, firm. She roused, asked for her glasses, listed down the hallway, her breasts swaying.

That left me with the guy. I wanted to stab him, burn him, make him pay. His pimpled butt. I pulled the sheet to his shoulder, then poured a glass of ice water on his neck. He bolted up, yelling. Then he saw me, and tried to figure out where he was. I could see him backpedaling, trying to return to a place where everything in this picture made sense.

"You need to go home now," I said.

"Okay," he mumbled.

"Now," I insisted.

He felt around for his jockey shorts, and I went into the kitchen. He dressed fast, I'd give him that much, and shut the front door as quietly as he could.

I was just reaching to get down the Cheerios when my little brother padded up behind me. I jumped.

"Hey, you scared me," I smiled.

"Who was that man?" John asked sadly.

"What man?"

"I got up to go to the bathroom. I saw them." And then he was crying. I held him and held him. "Why is this happening?" he asked.

"I don't know, honey. I just don't know."

Chena Night

Autumn, the quickest season in Alaska. As they have for centu-
ries, geese and cranes gather, then fly. Moose bulk up for the long
winter. After midnight sun, there's just enough darkness now to
think again of night.

The cow moose with twin calves swims our river, rises drip-
ping in the scant dark of August. They crop broccoli ground
level, take one bite of each cabbage. Rhubarb they leave, and
zucchini. Nightshade leaves survive. Before dawn, the river
covers their tracks.

Wherever they brush the trees, leaves turn gold.

∞

Two of my nieces come up from Arizona to help us home the second time from the hospital. On the morning I'm scheduled to be released, Joe goes to the airport to pick up Amy and Hanna. In anticipation, I shuck the hospital gown, and slip on a black T-shirt dress that used to fit. These machinations take planning, and odd contortions. My body protests, even at raising an arm, or trying to lift a garment.

When they come through the door, I'm in the wheelchair, itching to go. "See? Told you she'd be ready," Joe says.

Hanna rushes to hug me. Amy tells me later that she had to grab the doorframe. Her knees went weak when she saw me. She said, "I thought I was prepared. But you looked so vulnerable."

I've enjoyed abundant good health, so she hadn't any foreshadowing for this level of feebleness.

I'm not yet well enough to be angry. My nieces joke that the kid who hit us better not meet *them* in a dark alley.

∞

Who needs angels? I have avenging nieces, who have taken biology, and believe true justice compels them to track down the kid screaming illegally down the bike path, four-wheel ATV blind behind brush, split seconds before he tossed our lives like dice. The avenging nieces reason it's only fair—a spleen for a spleen. They're pretty sure once they've got him open, they can pick his out, and once removed seal it in a Mason jar, unvented for posterity.

∽

Joe sets a baby monitor beside the bed. I sleep on his side, closer to the bathroom. To turn in bed, to sit up, to reach for a drink of water, I need help. To go into the bathroom takes a strategy and an assistant. No position's without pain. But at least at home when I finally drop off, no one interrupts blessed sleep.

After the first few days, I make the huge effort to get up for breakfast. And that's the whole accomplishment for that day.

∽

Part of what I hated about the hospital was not being able to see out. More than aesthetic deprivation it was a matter of wanting to know that the world was still there, and that I might find a way back into it by finding my way out of this.

One of the first things I did when I got home was to make my slow way over to where I could look toward the Chena River. I couldn't focus yet, couldn't see the beaver swimming toward her lodge or the trees she gnawed to construct her home. But I could breathe in cool air that hadn't been worked on by machinery, could hold inside me the clouds.

I hobbled to the window, glad to see (though it was blurry) the river. Dark slash tipped with white swooped through the blue. "An eagle, look!" I cried. I was leaning on Hanna. She saw it, too. *Get real. That's a raven with a biscuit.* Potent sign, odd omen, laughter.

∽

Pintails, mallards, canvasbacks. Hairy woodpeckers. Ptarmigan, willow grouse. Redpolls. Trumpeter swans, tundra swans.

131

Herring gulls, mew gulls. Hawks. Eagles. Grebes. Chickadees, black-capped and boreal. Camp robbers. Ravens. Snow geese, Canada geese. Sandhill cranes.

∞

Around the house, I balance by leaning on walls or on a willing loved one. For doctor's appointments, we've rented a wheelchair again. The knee doctor tells me everybody in the emergency room was amazed that I pulled through. What is the appropriate response to that? Thanks?

What's the etiquette of survival?

Not to be ungrateful, but I plan to do better than that.

∞

A man I'd never met took out of me the traditional locus of anger—the spleen. But did you know some spleens travel with an entourage? My surgeon left the Spleenettes, backup do-wop singers who keep on humming.

∞

The first anger flares like a cleansing flame.

After that, anger takes too much fuel.

Or maybe it's an anchor, and I don't want to stay in this place.

∞

For most of my adult life I've not been a great fan of TV. All of a sudden, I get addicted to *Law and Order*. If three episodes air each day, I want to watch them all. As soon as they hear those distinctive seven notes, the nieces head out the door.

What am I letting in? The decisions aren't always just. In fact, the law has less and less to do with justice as people figure out how to work the system.

∞

When I'm ready to try to walk around the block, we take the wheelchair along in case I need to rest. Amy slips her hand into mine. Her long elegant fingers help me balance. I remember holding her hand when those fingers were pudgy, holding her hand just this way as she learned to walk, holding her hand later as we crossed a busy street, holding her hand when we took a sack of carrots to feed the goats and horses at the end of the block back in Arizona.

We take it slow and easy, this tentative workout as strenuous as any I've ever tried.

Amy and Hanna take turns pushing each other, and discover that able-bodied people avoid meeting the eyes of the one in the wheelchair. The nieces delight in saying hi, forcing the joggers to acknowledge them. If they were confined a little longer, they'd discover that people often "talk over" a person in a chair. My aunt Suzie says it irritates the hell out of her that people assume she's mentally defective when she's in her wheelchair. Often waiters ask my uncle Harry, "And what does she want?" Harry always says, "Better ask her."

∾

Maybe we cannot prepare, no matter how we try, for the essential changes in our lives.

Maybe nothing we can prepare for is life-changing.

∾

Some nerve. How marvelous in its complexity, a body that assigns to one nerve, the third cranial nerve, responsibility for the workings of the pupil, expanding and contracting, and for the lifting and closing of the eyelid. That same nerve controls muscles that move the eye itself. My particular hard whack on the head leaves this nerve palsied. The eyelid of the left eye just stays shut. If, with great effort, I force the lid open and like a weightlifter hold it suspended there, the eye can see fine. It just isn't coordinated anymore with what the right eye is doing. So vision is doubled and skewed.

For everyday tasks, like rising from a chair, I just use my right eye, so I can balance. The eye doctor says, "It's early yet. Too soon to say if it'll get better. Just use the eye whenever you can." I tell him what I want most is to read. He shows me how to tape up the lid so it won't be so exhausting to use the eye.

Not being able to read for more than a few minutes at a time scares the hell out of me. At first, it wasn't an issue, because I couldn't hold a book or stay awake long enough to make sense of a paragraph. But now I want to live among pages again.

∞

A poet at the university is taking a medical leave of absence. Colleagues call to see if I might like to teach a class. There's no way. (It's a good thing I'm retired—no way could I do my job.) This courtesy sets me thinking, though: Will I one day be able to follow a thought from start to finish? Will I read a whole book? Will I be able to hold poems in mind long enough to talk about them?

What will happen to my heart if I can't read?

∞

When I'm out of the wheelchair, we return to the scene of D.'s crime. We park where the ambulance did, on the gravel flats before you get to the slough, and crunch across to the bike path. Joe finds skid marks along the concrete divider.

"Here's where he hit the wall."

"Here's where you were lying."

"Here's where I landed."

It makes me queasy, being here. The alders still block the sight line. I step off the path.

∞

I wonder how his life has changed, the boy who hurt us. I wonder if it *has* changed. I wonder, but not enough to call him and find out.

శ

Sometimes, when nothing of substance is within my control, small insults really get to me.

The orthopedic expert writes that my broken ring finger displays "a hammer deformity." Deformity? I look at my finger and feel a wave of affection for it, bowing toward the palm.

I refuse his label. May I learn from this broken part of myself, this example close at hand. No matter how prideful my desires, it will never lift from its posture of humility.

శ

My friend Carol Houck Smith sends a care package of books, the best gift. I choose the galleys of Stephen Dunn's *Different Hours*, knowing it's a privilege to see these poems early. I feel like I'm getting away with something. Dunn writes, "A heart is to be spent." Heart wide open, I teach myself to read again.

I practice holding the left eyelid open with my hand, closing the right eye, and reading a page. "More and more you learn to live / with the unacceptable." Then I let the left lid drop, read a page with my right eye. Left again, then right. The eyes each offer separate clear images. Both eyes together produce hallucinations. It's slow, this new kind of reading. But that's okay. I'm taking my time. "Tell them I had second chances," Dunn says to his eulogist. Yes.

శ

Reading again, I tape open the hurt eyelid. I come upon lines Dunn writes about how we try to shove pain aside, lines he surely writes just for me:

Out of decency
we turn away, as if it were possible to escape
the drift of our lives, the fundamental business
of making do with what's been left us.

∞

Dena, the Victim Coordinator, comes to our house. (What a title! When she leaves, we make jokes—if you want a victim, call her up. If you want to *be* one, make sure she's got your number.) She tells us what to expect from the court system, what our rights as victims are. She asks us to fill out statements to be presented to the court, and leaves us the forms. Joe fills his out right away. I scribble mine maneuvering around the plastic splint taped to my broken finger. Hope the judge can read it.

∞

After a few weeks, in dim light, if I hold very still, I can almost reconcile both eyes' offerings. I brag to my niece, "You're in focus!" and Hanna laughs, saying, "So I shouldn't go like this, eh?" She shimmies into a blur of colors again.

∞

I remember liking to take off my glasses to look at the Christmas tree when I was a kid. Each light became a fuzzy circle of color, overlapping, washing into one another like water paints. Now it's as if I can't put the glasses back on at will.

The focus stays longest at the movies—dim lights, stillness. I watch through the best part of my field of vision, with my chin pointed up so I can look through the lower edges. One friend says ruefully, "The bad news is, there aren't that many movies worth seeing."

∞

I try hard to get an appointment with a researcher at Stanford specializing in damage to the third cranial nerve. After being thwarted repeatedly by their Byzantine phone system, I finally get a human being. He agrees to schedule a time, then says, "And your child's name?" It turns out the researcher is a pediatric ophthalmologist.

"*I'm* the patient," I say.

"Oh. Well, Doctor only sees adults one day a month. Let's see. She's booked through February." This is July. We live twenty-five hundred miles away. Forget it.

∞

As part of a game my nephew's making up as we go along, three-year-old Malik lifts my shirt. The stripe of my scar is still shiny and bright. He draws back, thinks it over. And then, like anyone who does not understand, he translates something foreign into something he knows. He tilts his head for a better look.

"Kitty scratch you?"

∞

Do we take scars as evidence of injury, or as evidence of healing?

Do we bear scars of one life? What about scars handed down, scars we pass along?

∞

One afternoon when Joe has gone to his hangar to scale the mountain of work piled up there, I wallow. All the things I can't do anymore, all the things I won't ever do. I call my hero, my aunt Suzie, who has never been completely well during her whole adult life. Lupus has kept adapting to whatever treatment the doctors can dream up. And now ovarian cancer.

We talk about tests, about cures that are worse than the ailments. We talk about her family's print shop, about writing, about Joe's devotion to me and my uncle Harry's devotion to her.

Then I ask, "So what if I don't get well?"

She's quiet a long moment, then says, matter of factly, "What if you don't?"

This sobers me. And I realize she's telling me that whatever comes, I'm going to have deal with it.

And because of her, I'm pretty sure I can.

༺

Outside the Rabinowitz Courthouse in Fairbanks a huge group mills around. It's early in the spring, and ice floes still skim down the river, but people are in track shoes and shorts, numbered bibs. They're stretching and bending, taking one last swig from water bottles.

Then an ambulance pulls away, and hundreds of attorneys and judges and clerks take off after it.

༺

Outside the courtroom, we wait to be called in. D.'s mother asks if they think my eye will ever open again. I tell her nobody knows. Her son's lawyer glances over, as if we shouldn't be talking.

D. stands close enough so I can overhear him stressing to his attorney that he had to take off work to come down here.

He looks a little bewildered by this whole court scene, as if he can't quite figure out what it has to do with him. I say to him, "This summer hasn't been any picnic for you."

He brightens. "You got that right," he says.

༺

It's faith, not disillusionment, that breaks our hearts.

༺

Healed, my right knee looks like a bad spackle job. The surface's uneven, the colors blotchy. About an inch below the kneecap, a shin divot—skin over bone, it feels like. The nerves tangle, tango. When I draw fingernails up the left side of the knee, I feel tingles cascading down the right side. It's an odd intimacy, like carrying on a conversation with an imaginary friend. A private sensual pleasure.

≈

Joe's bruised all over and his back's wrenched. My body can't turn or roll or bear any pressure. My right knee doesn't bend much, stapled together with wire. We reach for one another anyway. Tender and inventive, we manage.

≈

You have taken me to a place where ripe papaya let go their stems and fell, heavy with juice, in our hands. You have taken me fifty feet under, swimming with eagle rays, while humpbacks above us sang their way south. You have shown me the ancient madrona healed over barbed wire nailed decades ago to red bark. You have held me shivering before a flaring crosshatch of split oak. In a small plane you have lifted me over the San Juans, all of us citizens of the clouds. You have taken me to a house with windows to the sky, walls open to night. You have made me your home. You have taken me to the place mist barely conceals the next island, where each rise, veiled, each hollow opens, sacred.

≈

On September 22, three months and three days after the injury, my left eye opens, on its own. On the bedroom wall, a half circle of children has gathered to watch one girl light the fuse. Small celebration—one firecracker. All the kids have hands over their ears, except one big sister who holds her hands over her little brother's ears. The match is almost to the wick. I blink twice, three times. The faces in Wai Ming's picture stay in focus, faces fascinated with the world.

My eyes don't track exactly in unison, and they don't blink as one, but close enough. I can see the faces of those I love. I can look at art and at the river, at birds and trees.

I can read.

FOUR

∞

Constants

The artist Andy Goldsworthy has spent his life making art that disappears. He uses materials at hand to make sculptures outdoors, in natural settings. If his material that day is ice, the forms will last as long as the sun isn't too intense. If his material is leaves, the elegant ring he crafts around a hole will last until the leaves rot into new soil or blow away. Only photographs remain of his years of intricate work. Maybe those of us who work in stone, in words, only delay the inevitable.

1968, April

In American History, I'm lifting up my glasses so Mr. Koenig turns into a pinhead. He is telling us all the reasons war is good, this war in particular. Boys have to register. Some burn their cards.

Mr. Bee rushes in from the yearbook print shop, ink up to his elbows. "What are you going to tell them about King?" They lock eyes.

Mr. Koenig rolls the television cart to the center of the room. We see men on a motel balcony, pointing. In here, the air's thick with whispers. Outside, awake with April, mourning doves whirr so deep in the throat they almost choke.

1968, June

What kind of second chance is this, Bobby's running?
Too soon, we find out.

Typing

I didn't stop at the Circle K on the way home from school that day, didn't have a nickel for a Big Hunk, seven cents for a 50–50, twelve cents for sunflower seeds. I got home early.

Mom had somehow clean-and-jerked the ancient Olivetti, heavy as an anvil, out of its case and onto the Formica dinette. Hunched over the keyboard, she didn't hear me come in. At the end of each line, the bell dinged. She swiped the metal handle with her left hand, guided the carriage all the way right with one stroke of grace.

One line she tapped out slowly. Then she pushed herself, faster, faster. Behind her I could read, over and over and over:

The quick brown fox jumped over the lazy dog.
The quick brow fox jumped ove rthe laxy dog.
The quick brown fox jumped over the lazy dob.
The qick brown fox jumped over the laxy dob.
The quick brown fox jumped bover the lasy dov.
Now is the time for all good men to come to the aid of the party.
Now is the tiem for all good men to come to the aid ofthe party.

The letters jumped at her command, each snapping separately onto the striped ribbon, uncentered, the tall letters redheads. The letters jumped all together, their metal legs whacking into a clump.

Beside her, a chance at absolution, little circular eraser with a black brush attached at the center.

She concentrated like an archeologist brushing dust from evidence just unearthed. Took a deep breath. The eraser spent itself cleaning up the world, and still her errors showed. Words smudged under her fingertips. With one jerk, her right hand ripped the ruined sheet from the roller.

She deflated then, like a tent with its center pole kicked away.

"Just takes practice, that's all," I told her. "You're as good as anybody else."

"We need money now, kiddo. Who's going to hire me?"

From somewhere deep inside, ancient sounds forced their way out. Through her. The wail of the sabertooth pierced by the spear. The grinding scrape of glaciers carving out a new valley. The shriek of the exposed tree, split apart by lightning.

Lever

Her skin was so white you could see the pathways of her blood, just under the surface.

When asthma attacked, she sat at the edge of her bed, curling herself over the fist she pressed hard into her chest, as if there were a lever between her breasts.

When the lever stuck, she had to drag herself into the emergency room for a shot of adrenaline, her lips outlined in blue, her pallor an unearthly glow.

I came too, so I could talk when she couldn't. In the car, I sat close. It was my job to grab the steering wheel if she blacked out.

Her asthma meant no swimming, no matter how hot Tucson summers got, no matter if the heat bent the air till Our Mother of Sorrows swam into a blur of colors.

She kept her medicines out of reach, second shelf up, so she could reach but the little kids couldn't, a whole cupboard full, to keep her breathing, to keep her from diving, plunging.

For her main affliction, us kids, medicine offered no help.

Hiding under Poison Leaves

One night I couldn't take it, not one second more. I left, wondering if Mom would even notice. When it was 1:30 in the morning, almost time for her to come home, I walked down the arroyo to the clump of trees behind the swimming pool, a safe place even for a waitress's kid.

Before she left for the Lucky Strike I ironed her outfit—straight black indestructible skirt, low-cut ruffles on the K-Mart blouse. I hated the chore as she must have the job—toting beer to the leagues, Al Ball's Chevron, Addressograph-Multigraph. Once, I made her late. She came when I called, and held me, fought for me against some pure and adolescent pain. Most nights we couldn't afford it.

She'd bring home the best of a bad lot to dance till they fell, the crashing bodies payment against some larger debt. I'd yell, then cry most school nights till exhaustion tucked her in. But one night my anger rose past double-edged blades in the back bathroom. I uncapped the little white tube free from the Avon lady, Furious Passion, my color, not hers, and wrote in virgin lipstick three words on the mirror, then opened the window and left.

She held her lipstick smack against her mouth, one wide pull in each direction. She'd smear her lips against each other, then kiss a square of toilet paper, leaving always surprised a mouth.

Under the oleanders behind the public pool I waited for her to miss me. I knew she would yell *I know you can hear me* just like she used to when I was little and she said stay within hollering distance or else, and she did yell *I know you can hear me*, but I heard in her voice how much she did not know.

When she left, desperate, to wake up my friends, I walked home up the arroyo, sure the punishment would be swift.

Hood

If she's not going to care about me, why should I care? I walk home from high school angry, tired of setting the rules, enforcing the rules. I'm sick of being in charge.

A car pulls up beside me, slows down real slow. "Wanna ride?" Randy Toomey says it like a taunt, like he knows I won't. His hair's greasy, his shirt unclean. He's a hood, a dropout, a grownup almost.

"Sure," I say, and slide in the front. He drives around to a vacant lot, pulls into some shade.

"Whaddaya doin' way over there?" He reaches over and scoops my shoulders across the seat so I'm tucked into his armpit. I wince at his bad teeth. His mouth dives for mine, his lips devouring, his tongue digging in. Camel smoke, beer, Big Red gum, all swirled. He kisses like a starving man. Then he kisses like he wants to drown me. Two kisses are the limit of his politeness. Then he tries to cop a feel. I flinch away.

"I hardly know you," I protest.

"What, you want a story?" He's amused. "Ok. Here's something. Last night I took a carload of guys to the top of Mount Lemmon. We had a dare. We drove all the way down without lights and without touching the brakes. Anybody who tried to slow us down was a pussy. Whaddya think a that?"

I think you're all idiots, dangerous idiots. "Look, I've got to get home," I say.

"Not yet, you don't. Nobody's home and you know it." *How does he know that?*

He enjoys the little flicker of fear in my eyes. "Nah, you're gonna do some stuff and make me feel real good."

"I don't think so." I push away, try to open the door. He's locked it somehow from his side.

"You know you want it."

I don't dignify that with a word, a glance. I keep my head down and wait to throw an elbow, wait to aim a knee.

"Shit, I know a hundred girls got the same thing as you between their legs."

"So go see them."

"I got you." He's reaching over again, ready. He's strong. I try to keep my hair out of his grip, try to shield my body. Maybe if I throw up he'll leave me alone. He shoves his hand inside my shirt, twists one breast. I cry out.

A hard knock nearly shatters his window. I look up, glad to see the face of a policeman. He tells me to get out and go sit in his patrol car. He knows Randy by name, and gives him hell. He tells him that if he ever sees him around me he'll take him straight to jail.

When he gets back to me, his face is angry, stern. "Listen, Toomey has a record. He hurts people on purpose. He hits. He rapes. He's trouble all the way around. Where the hell are your parents?"

"I don't know." That's the truth.

The officer drives me home. He talks to me all the way. Our yard, the dirt and weeds. In all the time he talks to me, he never once says, "Don't."

Instead, he says, "Respect yourself."

Broken

That's part of what I still don't get. Mom had the empathy to notice the suffering of migrant workers, to try to ease the way of the poor. She had the imagination to put herself in the place of the women struggling to raise their kids in shelters made of boxcars or cardboard. She'd been bit often enough to remember how it feels. She did what she did to us anyway. So what broke inside her that let her hurt us? What gave up in her before she gave up and left us?

Does her hitting mean that she knew she was inflicting pain, she knew what pain feels like, and she just didn't care? Sometimes. Does her leaving mean she was so immersed in her own pain that she couldn't care? Sometimes. No one was helping her. No one was aware of her pain in ways that relieved it. No one was taking care of her, so she quit taking care.

Does this matter to anyone beyond the ones she hurt?

Yes, because she's everywhere, the mother who cannot cope, the mother grown hostile, she's everywhere, the one nobody's taking care of.

Toyota Trips

After the divorce my father and his drinking buddies all bought used Toyota Land Cruisers. They'd take them out in the desert and rip up great swaths of creosote and cactus.

At their best, these trips were loud, hot, dusty, dry.

One Saturday, I wanted to stay home, to hang out with my friends. Dad said, "You're coming. Get in."

I stared out the bleary plastic window, zipped up against blowing dust. We bounced over dips and divots, rat-patrolling. When we stopped for lunch, I dug around the ice chest. Coors, Bud, Michelob. "Where's the pop? Where's the water?"

"Guess we forgot." Dad didn't care. "Have a beer." The other kids laughed and popped triangles into their cans. They were twelve, ten, eight.

I hated him at that moment as much as I hated beer. It was desert, over one hundred, no shade. I tipped the ice chest and cupped a few swallows in my sweaty palm. I refused ever to go again.

Embarrassment

Long after the parents divorced, my dad showed up at 2:00 in the morning. On a school night, damn. He had four Hefty bags. "Get your stuff. Let's go," he said.

Mom had left us four months before to live with her boyfriend. She'd check in every few days, bring us food or lunch money. We hadn't seen Dad for months. Things were actually easier without the parents around. We'd been doing pretty well on our own.

"Look, we have school tomorrow. Can't this wait?" I asked. Dad was already married to Crazy Marcia. Nobody wanted to live at that house.

"The welfare people are about six steps behind me. Want them to take you to Mother Higgins?" That was the juvie jail. "Plus, it'll be embarrassing if the police get involved."

Dad was big on avoiding embarrassment. So was I.

I woke the little kids and we stuffed into black plastic what we couldn't stand to leave behind.

Don't Tell

My nickname in high school was "The Nun." I didn't smoke, drink, party. When the other kids conned some adult into buying their Boone's Farm, their whatever's-cheapest beer, when dozens of teenagers gathered at the end of Speedway for a boondocker, I drove out into the desert and dragged my siblings home.

Once, John nearly poisoned himself with Thunderbird. Green-faced, he stumbled out of the bathroom, and barfed foamy purple effluvium right in the middle of Dad's bed. He kept slurring, "Don't tell Dad, don't tell Dad."

"I think you just told him, buddy."

My siblings have each had trouble with alcohol.

So have I, but not by drinking it.

My Father's Wives #2

After the divorce, things slid downhill fast. Our whole household was an arroyo collapsing in on itself. Dad married Crazy Marcia, a bottle blonde with a serious affection for prescription painkillers. We nicknamed her daughters for their passions: the Nympho, the Pyro, the Klepto.

∝

Eating an orange at Marcia's house was a project. First, we'd post a sentry. Then one kid would lift an orange from the bowl on the table. That kid would walk fast into the bathroom. Everybody who wanted in on it came into the bathroom too. We'd peel the fruit, divide the sections exactly evenly (you cut and I choose), then swallow the fruit almost without chewing. We washed our hands and faces, brushed our teeth. We flushed the orange peels, wiped the counter.

When Marcia came out of her room in the late afternoon, she'd know right away that something had changed. She'd count and count the oranges. "Eight. There should be eight."

"Seven," we'd say. "This time you bought lucky seven, remember?"

∝

The day of the moonwalk I had a date. Chuck Quimby came early to pick me up. We couldn't leave the house, though, because Marcia had an episode. She had plucked out every hair in both eyebrows, and held a stencil high across her forehead to pencil in new ones. She couldn't get them right. Couldn't. Her hands wouldn't cooperate. Irritation slid into hysteria, and Marcia got clingy. I pictured techniques they taught in Junior Lifesaving, the ways to keep a panicked swimmer from drowning you too.

We erased the jagged arches over her perplexed eyes. We fed her crushed ice. Her face, bald and sallow, sank in on itself. She looked powdery, like the surface of the moon, marked by boots, by men.

Finally, she slept.

"One small step for a man . . ."

∞

For the first three days, I tried to convince Crazy Marcia that I really was sick. She accused me of loafing, of trying to get out of chores. She made me stay in my room and didn't allow phone calls. I could barely stagger to the john.

After six days, my sister got worried. I hadn't eaten, and didn't care anymore who believed me. "You have to take her to the doctor," Ginny told Dad. He was late to work. He flicked off her worries like dandruff.

After twelve days, the school called. My sister answered. "She hasn't been in school because she hasn't kept anything down for twelve days." Dad was really pissed that she told. But he came home from work, scooped me up, and took me to the doctor. Light as a dried cicada husk, I felt as though any stray breeze might whisk me away.

The doctor took one look and put me in the hospital. Hepatitis. "The yellows of her eyes should have given you a clue," he scolded. He kept me there, longer than he had to. He kept me there as long as he could.

∞

Marcia was being mean to John, the littlest one. For some imagined infraction, for not reading her mind well enough, she made him pull weeds for hours in hot sun, no breaks, no shade. My sister Ginny took him a glass of water. Marcia told her to pour it out.

"You bitch," Ginny glared.

Marcia began her campaign to kick Ginny out of the house. Relentless, she made sure Dad didn't sleep. Finally, he shoved out his own daughter, drove Ginny himself to a safer house.

Leaving

The bars locked up at 1:00 and the musicians and bartenders had one last drink after last call. Dad dragged in around 2:00.

John, his bed covered with a mound of laundry Marcia wanted him to do, fell asleep in the living room. Dad headed for the organ, wanted to try a new embellishment on "The Russian Saber Dance." He could hear it in his head, "Da-duh-duh-duh-duh-duh-duh-duh-duh-DUH-da!" His toe snagged on John's sneaker and he almost fell.

He caught himself on the organ bench, then turned. Marcia was standing near the window, backlit by a blade of moon, looking down at John. With both hands she was gripping the handle of a butcher knife.

This would be a good time to take off, Dad decided. He woke us up, and we grabbed a change of clothes. It was a school night. We left Marcia pleading. We left Marcia's daughters there. Dad drove us to the airport. We weren't going anywhere, he just wanted pie. It was good. Then we went to Lainie's house. Lainie was a singer and my Dad played bass. She was his friend, our friend, too wise to be his lover.

The third night at Lainie's house, my boyfriend and I were doing homework. Urgent ringing, pounding, kicking at the door. We opened it to find a woman crouching over so her shirttail might cover her nakedness. It didn't quite. Her head wounds gushed. We led her into the bathroom and bolted the door behind us. I gave her my robe. We called the cops.

"My baby. My baby. My baby," she burbled through her broken teeth.

When the police got there, she told them her baby was still

over there, still in the house with her husband who had torn down a birdcage and used the wrought iron rod it swung from to bash her.

One of the officers asked three times whether she really wanted to press charges. "Yes," she said. "This time, yes."

The police went and got him and tucked him gently into the back of the patrol car.

We gave her cold water, ice, a pillow for the night. A doctor she refused.

The next morning all that was left was one word—thanks—scrawled in second grade penmanship across a page in my notebook.

Four days later we saw her in K-Mart. Four days later, her husband was yanking her by the arm down the aisle.

Not Now

I remember the last time I saw my mother. I went to visit on Davis Monthan Air Force base, where she was living with her lover, a sergeant named Mac who actually smiled when he referred to her as "my soiled dove." I told her we all missed her, terribly. I showed her the Capezio shoes I'd bought with baby-sitting money. I told her what each of the little kids was up to. I didn't mention Dad or Crazy Marcia.

I wanted to ask her things. My boyfriend kept putting his hands inside my clothes. I didn't want to stop him. Did that mean I was a bad person? Did that mean we were in love? But she was in no shape for questions. I invited her to come see my chorus concert at the high school.

She had been bedridden for a month. The doctors said there was no reason she shouldn't be recovering. I wanted to give her some reason to smile, some reason to get up. I told her she needed to stay curious about the world. Didn't she want to know what was going to happen to us? In all my teenaged self-righteousness, I told her, "You've got to justify your existence." And she said, "Not now. I'm tired." She turned her face to the wall, worked hard for her next breath.

A few days later, my uncle broke the news.

"Your mother expired last night."

I wanted to scream, "She's not a subscription!"

The doctors called it heart failure, and that's true. She didn't have the heart to stick around. She just plain didn't want to be here.

Lips

My mother had a luscious mouth, sumptuous. A venomous neighbor, angry about something else, sneered, "You have nigger lips." My mother looked her directly in the eyes: "Why, thank you!" she said gently. The neighbor, disarmed, didn't know what to do.

Just because Sue couldn't stand spit, my mother gathered slobber between her big lips and slathered Sue's thrashing face. Good night!

In her coffin, my mother's lips looked like wax, Halloween lips without red dye number 2. Someone had brushed on a dry orange color, outlining a prim little mouth inside the edges of her lips.

Wires held open her nostrils. Her lips were stitched shut, not very neatly. The undertaker's hairdresser couldn't do much with my mom's thin hair, hair she called ww hair, World's Worst. Each fine strand lay flat against her skull. Her hands, crossed over her chest, posed like carved suet.

Why did they put the family behind a curtain, like the zonk prize on *Let's Make a Deal*? After everyone else had filed out, the man with the black suit and funny smell motioned that we should walk down a little hallway that led back to the mortuary chapel.

It was there, yawning open, the ridiculous box. We paid way too much, money we didn't have, though water and worms would eat through fancy wood just as easily as plain. My uncle, guilty, had refused my mom a five hundred dollar loan. She was drinking heavily, and he was probably right not to bail her out again. So he almost went for the concrete-lined vault. I had to say, out loud, "We don't need that." The man with the funny smell fixed me with a look.

And there it was, her body. It held me once, then pushed me sixteen years ago out into this world. It hit my sister Ginny every day, and the rest of us when we didn't get out of the way. It cradled each of us, as if we were miracles. It was sexed and sexed and very little loved by men. It was a constant source of confusion for those of us who loved the woman it held. We never knew if that body would be on our side or if it was another threat, disguised as Mom.

Evergreen

Ever after, a limo would stand for waste, horror, somebody so beaten down she pounded her rage into her children, then pounded herself into the ground.

On the day of her funeral, cops stopped traffic. Where were they going, all those drivers acting as if this were just another day?

I tore white lace off my only dark dress, washed and ironed outfits for the little kids. For Mom I'd picked a dress I'd never seen her wear, orange and brown, strange dress shoved in the back of the closet, so it would be harder to picture—my mother under ground.

Satin sheets made me furious. Why now? She never rested on satin when she was breathing. But my uncle, guilty, insisted. Coffin showroom, dim and cool, no windows. Swamp music, no words, no harmony.

Graveside, I stood at the edge of her deepening distance widening into earth.

Her husband, our dad who had left us, didn't know where to put his hands. His hands never hit us. He barely knew we were alive. *He's what's left*, I thought. *He's what we have left.*

He's a substitute teacher who doesn't know where we are in the book, doesn't have any training in the subject. Asking anything of him feels like leaning on a wheeled cart, the projector plugged to the wall. Any pressure and it glides, what we have to lean on, away. Before long, the movie jerks to a halt.

Mom couldn't protect herself. She couldn't protect us from herself. She couldn't protect us from what was coming.

Thirty-five years pass. On the phone my sisters laugh the hard laughs that keep us partway sane. Ginny tells me, "Yeah, Sue said,

'It's a good thing Mom died when she did, or she'd have really fucked us up.'" Ginny laughs hard, waits for me to laugh too.

I can't breathe.

Fresh grief—for her, who did what she could, not enough.

Fresh grief—that anyone close to her could be glad she died.

Fresh grief that still I can't protect her.

Fresh grief that still I can't protect them.

Fresh grief that their hurts will never die.

Bananas

After my mother's funeral, when my siblings needed to be sure of the truth, they'd demand, "Swear on Mom's grave?" I couldn't stand it, couldn't stand to hear it, couldn't stand to see it in my mind again.

I told the other kids I never wanted to hear that again. At first, that just made them say it more. After enough badgering though, the kids agreed on a code that meant "Swear on mom's grave?"

So we shifted. When we were pretty sure one of us was lying, we'd tilt our heads and ask gravely, "Bananas?"

Outsiders couldn't imagine the gravity of that tropical fruit.

Remember

I remember writing the thank you notes after my mother's funeral. My great-aunt Jean wrote, "It's such a shame Hanna was cut down halfway through her life."

Sixteen years old, I thought, "Well, she was pretty old, thirty-five."

∞

Playing "remember when" with my siblings means eventually we'll argue. We were all there. Nobody's willing to give up a version held so long . . . I remember, Ginny remembers, Sue remembers, John remembers.

What about what I need for them to fill in, but they didn't notice? What about what they're counting on me to hold on to for them, but I didn't have room at that moment?

∞

"What do you remember of my mother?" I ask my uncle's childhood friend. He thinks for a while.

"Well, she was older, and really really pretty. Hmmm. Mostly, I remember she was kind."

∞

Marion Baker says, "I hated how your mom dumped you kids on Harriet. Your grandma never told Hanna *no*. It wasn't right."

Then Marion told me about how she and Grandma were band mothers together, running the concession stand to raise money. After ball games, they'd sit and laugh at the kitchen table, drinking pot after pot of strong black coffee, smoking cartons of Marlboros, counting out and rolling mountains of coins.

Locket

One of the few objects handed down to me when my mother died is a small rectangular locket engraved with a spray of wildflowers. Might be gold, might be plate, I don't care. It was hers. In her high school graduation portrait it rests in the hollow between her new breasts, nestled in folds of angora. Inside, a miniature photo of her, very young, her smile wide as the Milky Way. On the other side, all sleek muscles and slicked back Wildroot hair, grins a boy, a young man barely, cocky, and sure he's good looking so why not cut his eyes at the camera, why not lean back on two legs of his chair, the sun's out, he's got gas money and a pretty girl, surf's up man.

During the long fifteen years of their marriage, my parents yelled at each other, didn't even agree on a topic, just yelled in general. I took solace in the knowledge of that young man, imagined he was my real dad, lost to war or adventure, his presence there next to her heart a repudiation, male and sexy, of every reproach my father could throw at her. The self she carried in that locket grinned, eternally joyous, sassy as a skirt of giant kelp, stinging bare midriff and thighs, salty as her first good kiss, not shared with my father. Nobody recalls that boy's name now, not my grandmother, not my mother's high school friends, not Uncle Harry.

And my father, what did he carry, man with no amulet to protect him, and the heavy freight of his Nazarene father always on his shoulders. Pressed down on his knees in surrender to a God he never really met, my father shook off his father's zealous palm and knelt between the knees of any willing female. "Never pass up a chance at pussy," he told Harry, who knew even at thirteen there was something basic wrong with that advice. He wasn't sure what though because all the other guys were laughing and nodding, blowing smoke rings and French inhaling. He was the youngest one there, and counted himself lucky to be allowed to tag along. So Harry swallowed hard, he told me, swallowed the hard knot in his throat and made himself think about motorcycles, baseball, ham, pistachios, anything but how his sister's, my mother's, face would look when she found out who she'd married.

Hillclimb

I can't remember anymore my mother's laugh, can't recall the exact sound, only that it was loud and harsh and lasted forever, har-harring its crude way across Johnny's so everybody stopped chewing, and with fries poised one end coated red, turned to look.

No container for that laugh, no handkerchief, no hand-thrown mug, no galvanized bucket, no rough-lumber shed, no oleander churchyard, no glass-stained sanctuary. No shallow grave, no arroyo, no secret ravine. No bowl of mountains, no wall to wall carpet, no greasewood, ironwood, palo verde, mesquite.

That laugh broke the sky, blue white shatter light, burnt crack of one world lost, piercing laser of new worlds laid open. Thundercloud-heart backlit, dusty earth-heart wide open and bare. That laugh with a touch of molasses, touch of delight once innocent as red-brown rainwater gushing in gutter-streams over ankles of little kids making up songs in their own languages, once clear as rain-drenched air after heat so tight the inner membranes of nose and throat thinned to parchment, blood hieroglyphs dancing, shadow puppets jerked around behind the scrim.

Then the rush—menses, nosebleed—iron-salt taste of blood, our own blood, hers so close to the surface the simple kind gesture of stopping her from stepping in the path of a speeding Duster left five deep blue prints. And the unkind gestures lingered, spread purple, yellow, crushed side of windfall lemon no one could salvage.

That blood, that frail surface passed down till one day in the desert against the backdrop of screaming Greeves and Ducati, my unfaithful father and his delinquent buddies ripped up fragile slopes steep enough to flip cycles backwards. I rooted for the hills, not the hill climbers. As my father revved and revved, flailed against and fell back from the lip of the summit, my blood could not stay inside one more moment. Down my shirtfront, between my legs, head back, down my throat, ice held to the bridge of my nose. Her voice annoyed, saying we should cauterize. My visions of the tool, what tool? What tool to burn delicate places we want to be tougher? And how could it help, hellfire aimed toward the brain, help to cool blood flooding, the lusty slapstick of blood undammed and breathless? The throat exposed, hard swallows, the high drama of dailiness. The great gulps of blood laughs that hurt to see, to hear.

Nobody could survive such laughter. She didn't. Neither did I. We both died, one to the other, as she drifted far beyond where any hand could reach her and I grew into the woman her bruises, her laughter, guaranteed I'd be.

Estate

My last year of high school, I take four classes each day, then rush to work at the bank. I work as a relief staffer, filling in a few hours for people ill or on vacation. Today I'm at the New Accounts desk at the branch at Broadway and Olsen. A man protesting the war calls in and says, "I left a bomb in the Arizona Bank on Broadway." How setting a bomb is anti-war I can't figure out. We escort out the customers, do an emergency lockdown, then file out into bright sunshine. Police with dogs go inside. The bomb squad stands by. Nothing. They find nothing at any of the branches.

We're allowed back in, but it still feels weird, knowing somebody could so easily do harm. Mr. Stoddard stops by my desk. He was the victim of a hit-and-run driver who left him to die. Massively disabled now, he jerks and starts across the waxed floor, his forearm crutches awkward, splayed. His occupation now is driving out to I-10, picking up hitchhikers, and taking them wherever they want to go—St. Louis, Canada, New York. I mention that this might not be too safe. He works hard to tell me he's no threat to anybody.

"No. Somebody might hurt *you*."

"What duh duh duh ya think I have ta ta ta lose?"

I notice that the bank manager is getting edgy, impatient. He calls me into the back. I excuse myself, and go behind the teller's cages into the bookkeeper's cubicle.

"Stay back here and file checks for a while," the manager tells me. He doesn't want Mr. Stoddard to take up staff time. How ungenerous he is, this manager, a fat man who barely escaped his family's undertaking business. Such a ruse would never occur to his second in command, the assistant manager who can't spell. He drafts the letters he wants sent, scribbling when he doesn't know a word. "You know what I mean," he says. And I do.

So I open one of the little half drawers and take down a bundle of "work," checks encoded and processed, cancelled. I'm halfway through, filing fast by account number. A familiar name. What is this? Estate of Hanna Zoe Howe. My mother. Breath jerks. Pressure builds in my throat, behind my eyes. She's been dead now for nearly a year. That doesn't make this horse hoof to the gut any easier. What estate? The signature on the checks is that of a local attorney, a regular at the bank. Who hired him? What assets did he guide through probate? The six checks total about a thousand dollars—a fortune to my mother at the end of her life. I think of the tight-lipped woman at the Chinese market who made sure we ate when we couldn't pay. There's no check made out to her.

Stone

Hanna Zoe, because you died so often when I was a child I must go back there to the crippled mesquite with your eyes in it, to all the head-on crashes that did not kill you, to the barbed wire and sand of your voice, wheezing hard *Don't go too far.* You left us milk money in a can. We left you under a stone with no last name, unwilling to burden you in death with your unbearable life. Who were you then? Who are you now? Did you know your father came to see me on the night he died, came to my bed and held me, told me he was going? I had so much to ask I forgot to tell him to touch your face that way that made you stop for a moment, in peace.

Ice River

In May, when the Chena's completely open, all the ice gone from the banks by our house, an ice dam upriver gives. A whole new breakup—huge floes blunder downriver, gouging up whole trees. A layer of crushed ice shushes and slushes, three nights floating by. A lone Canada goose surfs on a pitching floe. The stories of our lives recur—lives human or water, earth or air. The fire crackles, each flame consuming branches, oxygen. The first grasses, nourishing enough to sustain winter grizzlies just roused, green up. Birch leaves, as one, burst out, flare, catch the breeze. Violent, ungainly changes. Each spring a recovery.

༄

Dr. Martino, the neurologist, asks me to perform a few small tasks. First he tells me three things to remember—sailboat, button, shoe. Then he asks me to walk heel to toe across his office. I'm bad at this, and list far enough to one side that I have to grab twice at the exam table. He checks my reflexes. I catch the little rubber hatchet before it thunks the broken places on my right knee. Looking deep into my eyes, he tells me what he knows about the third cranial nerve. Hard to predict if and when it might mend. He asks me not to look at what he places in my hand. Wild leaps, electrical, chemical, from fingertips to brain to lips. I say, "Penny. Paperclip. Key. Rubber band."

What could be more simple? Until the day we cannot do this. What then do we hold in our hand?

The least injured part of me wants to look him straight in the soul, this doctor of missed connections, and say correctly, "Shooting star. Red aurora. Mist forest. Life after this. Life."

He describes how the body rewires itself after insults to the brain. Most of my infarcts occur across the back of the brain, along the base of the skull, home to balance and memory. The one dead spot at the front of the brain may affect decisions, judgment. I glance at Joe, at my nieces, and know by their almost grins that I'm in trouble. "It's that judgment thing . . ."

Dr. Martino asks me to remember those objects he mentioned at the beginning of the exam. I think. I picture my great-grandma Langley's buttonhook, and recall button, shoe. And just as the sun sets, drifting out on a twilit Fijian lagoon, that sailboat.

Great mysteries, how we take in, sort through, retrieve, release each moment millions of bits of stimuli. How each of us hoards a ragtag collection that makes us exactly us, no one else.

At the first hearing, the judge rips into the prosecutor and the rep from the juvenile court. Why isn't this case being remanded to adult court? The accused is seventeen years old, and the injuries he caused are serious. He's charged with two counts of assault. The presumptive sentence in adult court is five to twenty years. I look over to see how this registers. D.'s mother blanches. D. doesn't seem to get it. This scares me as much as the idea that he might spend many years in jail.

And why is he still driving, the judge asks. His attorney mentions that his driving record is clean. Except for this one small incident, the judge counters, contemptuous. Then he makes a comment that haunts me. "If this young man had been Native, he'd be in adult court for sure."

Nobody has talked to us about this decision. The prosecutor protests that it wasn't her call. The rep from the juvenile court directs everyone's attention to the written conditions for release. Does the judge consider them reasonable?

Essentially the conditions say that until his trial, D. must act like a human being. No drugs or drinking. He must go to work every day. (He has dropped out of school.) He has a curfew. He's not allowed to drive a four-wheeler or snow machine. If any officer of the court or any law enforcement person asks, he must submit to drug or alcohol testing.

Pro forma, the defense attorney pleads not guilty on D.'s behalf, to give her time to prepare his case. Everyone accepts the conditions as stated, until the next hearing. As we leave the courtroom, D.'s family apologizes again. D. slouches, stares at his scuffed sneakers. He almost meets our eyes. Then, as if he's missed his central cue, D. apologizes too.

∞

A new fear—being alone. I've always carved out times to be by myself, to think, read, write. And now I'm scared. Had I been alone when the clot reached my lungs, I'd be dead now.

Joe has a new fear too—it takes a few months before he can leave me. When he's ready, I'm ready. Scared, but ready.

What I do from here on is a new coming-of-age story, a spiritual breaking away, the bildungsroman of middle age.

∞

Another new fear—stairs. I don't know why exactly, but it's about twice as hard to balance going down as it is going up. If I hold on tight with both hands on the rail and put both feet on the same level before I move to the next step, I can manage. Slow, shaky, scared.

At an afternoon reception on the university chancellor's lawn, I need to go down four stone steps. Flowerbeds cascade on either side, no railings. I might as well be on the platform attached to a tight rope. Stranded, I pause and survey the crowd, awaiting my knight. Joe breaks from his conversation, and eases me down, stepping backwards as I step ahead.

∞

The first time I venture alone out of the house, Joe's on his way home. He'll pick me up, and we'll go where my eyes feel most at ease—to the movies. I step carefully over rocks that might turn an ankle, watch for dips or holes along the verge. I'm excited to make it three whole blocks, and stand on the corner ready to wave.

This is going to be a surprise for Joe, so of course he's not watching for me. I see him coming along Farewell, and start waving early. Wave! Wave! Both arms WAVE!

Joe blows by, and I have to laugh. I turn around and hobble home.

By the time I get there, he has yelled for me, frantically searched all our rooms, the garage, the place we stack the stuff we can't sluff off.

It takes a while to kiss away the panic.

❧

We hear secondhand that some of D.'s teachers considered him "Most Likely to Harm Others." I guess he's been wild since he was little. Is this rank gossip? Is this useful information?

❧

My friend Frank tells me, much later, this. Hear it in his slow Virginia mountain drawl. "Remember that night you were fixing to die? Well, Eli and Emile had a concert. We had all gathered up at the school when word came that you were in bad, bad shape. Nobody could concentrate on the music after that, though the kids tried hard. So, on top of everything else, Peg, you ruined a perfectly good concert."

❧

Frank has no memory of saying that. In fact he's faintly horrified that I think he said such a thing. And I remember laughing hard when he told the story, which he's pretty sure I made up.

❧

Maybe Christ or Mohammed or the Buddha might think first of the neediness of those who do them harm. I'm not there yet.

I do wonder what D. was running from the afternoon he hit us.

I wonder if my father has stopped running or just slowed down.

I wonder what my mother thought her life meant. I wonder how she saw her place in this world.

❧

The Victim Coordinator tells us we may write a letter to the judge. It's not my call what happens to D. I obsess about it anyway. How should the court treat a kid whose thoughtlessness almost killed us?

179

For justice to be done,

1. D. must comprehend the severity of his crimes.
2. D. must take responsibility for his actions.
3. D. must change his behavior.

Toward these ends, we believe D. should be held account-able for hurting two people, nearly killing one. He should face two counts of assault. There is no way that his acts are misdemeanors, and he should not be allowed to plead down to one, or to have one count dismissed. It is not in D.'s interest for him to think that he can bargain his way out of serious crime. It is certainly not in society's interest. The state should not allow him to think his acts have little consequence.

To take responsibility, D. should pay restitution in the amount of $1,400 to help replace the bicycles and helmets he destroyed. D. should be aware that our medical bills will top $150,000.

If the law allows, D. should forfeit his ATV, and the pro-ceeds of its sale should be used to improve bike path safety.

To change his behavior, D. should do community ser-vice that requires him to develop compassion. For instance, tutoring an elementary school child who has trouble read-ing might allow him to practice thinking about someone other than himself.

D. could also do community service related to bike path safety. Specifically, he could trim back the shrubs and trees that block the sight line on the stretch of the bike path where he ran into us.

To help him become aware of how violence affects oth-ers, he could be required to help people who have been victims of accidents. He could do chores, help with therapy, and just get a clue about how long the recovery process can take.

In general, D. should not be allowed to operate any motor vehicle until he is nineteen years old. D. can get to work by walking, riding a bicycle, or catching a ride with friends or relatives. His attorney and his parents may try to say that this is a hardship. No. This is an inconvenience. A hardship is having a ventilator breathe for you, as Peggy did for two days during her weeks in the hospital. A hardship is having eyes that do not focus properly, as Peggy's have not since D. caused her injuries. Because of his crime, Peggy cannot drive. It is outrageous that D. should.

D. says he is "working on" his GED. He should have deadlines for each of the five tests. It would be reasonable to set a one-year deadline for D. to finish all five exams. (This gives him time to take them more than once, if need be.)

D. should be sentenced to time in a juvenile facility, with the sentence suspended, and probation until he turns nineteen years old. This gives him an opportunity to mature, but also gives him incentive to control himself. His attorney may say that D. is not a danger to others, but the facts prove otherwise. He was a danger to Joe, and he was a great danger to Peggy. If D. violates the conditions of his probation, he should serve time in the juvenile facility.

∞

In Alaska, there are two categories: Alaska and Outside. We've been grounded since June. In October, Joe needs to make an appearance at the International Mining Congress, held once every five years. This time, his father is being inducted posthumously into the National Mining Hall of Fame. So we need to go Outside. Travel from Fairbanks to Seattle, then out to Whidbey Island I handle fine. We rest there for a few days, and then catch the flight to Las Vegas.

By the time we get from Whidbey Island to SEA-TAC Airport, I am winded. Here's why: we shower and have a quick breakfast. After tucking the last few items into our luggage, Joe loads the suitcases in the car. We drive to the Clinton terminal, catch the ferry to Mukilteo, and join the throng headed south on I-5.

This alone takes most of the day's energy, plus the little bit I keep secretly in reserve.

We leave the car at the park-n-fly lot, climb (two tall steps up, scary) into the shuttle. At the airport, we check in at the kiosk, and trek toward the gate. We packed light, and each of us pulls one small rolling case. Joe offers to pull mine, but I want to do it myself. A few gates before our gate, the floor sweeps upward. I lean on the rail. Don't ask me why it never occurs to us to ask for one of those beeping carts, but it doesn't. I need to believe I am better. I need to believe I am better than I am.

Sisyphus, only sweaty and weak, I stand at the rail trembling. Joe has pulled ahead. By the time he notices I'm not near, I've bogged down in misery. Face to the wall, I cry like a fool just because I can't pull a suitcase up a ramp.

Angry at my own weakness, my own tears. Worried that the

182

throbbing in my knee means I've already done too much, and have hurt again what isn't healed. Ashamed that I am holding Joe back.

I doze in the plane, between announcements and coughs, rattling carts and too-loud conversations.

∞

When we make it to Vegas, where everything's elaborately fake, I can't fake anymore. I find a place to sit down while the luggage circles. We tumble into a cab.

When we get to our hotel, Joe jumps out to see to the luggage. The taxi is a small SUV, pretty high off the ground. I try two or three ways to get down. Then, hanging on to the doorframe, I aim my good leg toward the curb. The hurt leg bends, more than it has in months.

I don't fall down. I wobble to a column, lean there crying. The doorman, very concerned, asks if he can help. No. I scan for Joe. He helps me into the surreal lobby, row after row of slot machines, garish neon, the circles of hell.

Some of the elderly players insert cards instead of coins and sit there tethered to chance. Joe plunks me down right under a sign that says the stools are for players only. He goes to check in.

In a few moments, he comes back. Our room isn't ready. I lose it again. We weave to the restaurant. Over huge bowls of udon noodles I can't stop weeping. It's not pain anymore. It's wanting not to be here. Ever.

The people at the surrounding tables do a pretty good job ignoring us. I guessed meltdowns happen here more often than in real life. Joe leaves a big tip.

Our room is still not ready. We find friends from Fairbanks, Warren and Joan. They offer hugs and their room. We ascend twelve floors, and I sink into welcome oblivion.

∞

From all over the world, miners have gathered here to gawk at 350-ton trucks and the world's largest dozers. The promo for one German shovel shows an entire kindergarten class, teacher included, in the bucket.

We're here because Joe's family has helped a whole region prosper. Joe's dad, an Italian immigrant, came up to work the coal fields in the 1930s. He broke his back in the underground mine. When he healed, the company put him back to work long enough to prove he could work, then according to the wisdom of the day, fired him. He took on a contract making supporting timbers for the mines.

During World War II, the military wanted more than one source of coal, so they gave Emil a contract he could work with one crew, one truck, one tractor.

Joe's dad built the business—Usibelli Coal Mine—and helped build up the town of Healy. A few years after the man who had fired him was killed in a mining accident, Emil bought up that operation.

The same day the Good Friday Earthquake hit Alaska in 1964, a scraper operator missed a gear. His machine slid downhill, and Emil was crushed. Joe was en route back to Alaska from Palo Alto, where he was going to grad school at Stanford. At the Canadian border, a note from the family attorney waited—*Contact me re: your father's death.* That was the first Joe heard of it.

All phone lines were down. He tried radio. Desperate, he called the Red Cross. Their advice: Send a letter.

The mine Emil started now employs 125 people, and provides fuel to generate electricity and heat for Fairbanks and the Interior, and for export.

This award ceremony honoring his father matters, to Joe, to me, to his whole family, and to the mine's employees. After a rest and a shower, I'm glad we came.

The next few days I let Joe walk the trade show to kick tires on the Big Iron and to schmooze while I read, rest, recover. Las Vegas isn't so bad if you have several good books.

⚮

At the next hearing, my sister Sue comes with us. In the hallway, we introduce her to D. and his family. Sue doesn't want to shake their hands, I can tell. Sue is perfectly capable of yelling, perfectly capable of picking D. up by the scruff and shaking him hard. Her glare sears into him. He flinches, turns away.

There's a new prosecutor. The judge asks again why this case is in juvenile court. The prosecutor says she had no part in that decision. Each side sets out the facts as they see them.

There's remarkably little disagreement. D. has accepted responsibility for the two charges of assault.

Joe and I are asked to speak. We've learned that in the juvenile justice system, there's no suspended sentence, so D. will either receive probation and consequences or he'll go to jail. Joe begins by saying that he doesn't believe D. deliberately set out to hurt anybody. The judge stops him, and says, "Excuse me, sir, but the law makes no such distinctions."

I think about this. And to me it does make a difference. If he was reckless and self-absorbed and destructive that's terrible. But if he deliberately set out to cause harm, that's another level of evil. How much of this crime stems from immaturity? How much from intent?

I tell the judge that D. clearly needs to change his behavior, to think of other people, and to learn compassion. I tell him that I don't know enough about the juvenile jail to know if D. would learn compassion there, but I doubt it.

⚮

I have been trying and failing all my life, trying hard to make peace, to live in peace, to make a world where peace can thrive.

Sue says, "Maybe it's not one of your talents." She doesn't understand how failing just means I should try harder. I annoy her. I carry on.

∞

It's not peace when we watch what we say for so long we don't know anymore what we think. It's not peace when we make ourselves small so this moment's violence passes over us. It's not peace when words eat into us like acid and we try not to flinch. It's not peace when we're invisible. It's not peace when anybody is disposable.

∞

Three months later, at the adjudication hearing, D.'s attorney makes the case that because D. has landed a job that requires driving, it would be counterproductive to take away his driving privileges. This rankles a little. I couldn't drive for months. It's outrageous that D. should. The judge makes the law clear—in juvenile court, the consequences cannot be simply punitive but must have some direct connection to the kid's offense. The law does not allow the court to revoke a driver's license unless the crime involves driving a car. Because four-wheelers don't require licenses, the judge cannot restrict D. in this way.

The judge commends D. for the progress he has made the last few months, working a steady job, staying out of trouble, working on a GED. (A nasty little part of me thinks, "Give him a medal, why don't you! Jeez.") The judge emphasizes to D. that this is a huge second chance, and not to blow it.

∞

Once, when I was working as a poet in the schools, an eight year old wrote, "If I had a third eye, I could see the day of my death." I asked him why he wanted to see that. He said, "So I could prepare."

As if.

FIVE

Constants

My grandmother kept teaching me to read, all her life. She read to me about Yertle, the greedy dictator turtle. She and that red hen taught me to do my share. When we got bored, she made up new stories to go with the pictures. You'd be amazed at what we pulled up out of McElligot's pool. She always had another story. She read every day, two or three newspapers, bundles of letters, novels and stories and poems.

Once she sent me, long before any of my friends had read it, Milan Kundera's *The Book of Laughter and Forgetting*. Her note: *This book is exquisitely written, but the main character has an overactive penis.*

The Provider

Both arms around your waist, I buried my face in the cracked
black leather of your jacket. The throaty Harley leaned too
far, throttle cranked, hot pavement chewing up our footpegs.
Any stray patch of gravel, suicide. Scabby saguaro lurched by,
lean and wounded, never young. You loved pure speed, that
bike, and me, though I had no way to see it then. I was fifteen,
amazed at my body and amazed at you, all six foot six shut-
ting down (with one look) whistles and hot talk as we eased
blinking out of the desert and into the Beachcomber. Shut
down everybody, then turned for the first time to look at me
not as your elbow or toe, there all the time, easy to bump, but
the woman me, the one so far away I'd left before you noticed
I could run.

My showing up slowed you down, made you trade in your
tunes, your bike, your axe—your life a down payment on
mine. We both got took. You soured selling Chevys and office
machines. I took care of the little kids.

Once, I brought a college friend to your house. Your fourth
wife sang with you "Bad, Bad Leroy Brown" and "One Note
Samba," you clunking along on the clavinet, those canned
drums thumping like tired pistons.

It was 10:30 in the morning. A pitcher of salty dogs already
loosened your joints. We sat on the red velvet overstuff still
shrouded in double-duty plastic.

"George Wallace," you said. "The only clear choice."

I left.

Father, I am ashamed how ashamed of you I've always been when I know so little and that little learned by leaving.

Your absence has carved in me a place that healed like a cactus shoe—hard, fragile, secret—the deepest gashes shelter for some bounding pack rat or startled cactus wren.

Corsages

For years, I believed that my best friend's big sister really had gone to Texas to take care of her grandmother. She stayed away all summer and half a school year. When she got back, she was a lot older than when she left.

I wonder if she ever found the baby she never got to hold. I wonder if the baby found her. I wonder if the boy, whose parents ran a flower shop, a boy who before and after brought her cymbidium orchids, objected. I wonder if anyone even asked him what he felt. Those orchids, for every dance, calyx and corolla, their subtle seductive furls at her breast. He brought them because they were expensive and he wanted to impress. He brought them so maybe she'd let him touch her. He brought them after as sympathy flowers, ephemera for sorrow everlasting.

Gasp

One night at the double-feature drive-in I knew. It was time. After months kissing, caressing, pushing to the edge of the forbidden and just a little further, I sat up in his pickup and looked straight into my boyfriend's baby blues. He'd been sucking my nipples. Gently, then a little too hard, then gently. Two hours, no intermission. Our hands busy below. Every cell in my body wanted more, wanted something I couldn't do alone.

My respectable Villager, the dress I saved for, I lifted over my head. My skin shone in the moonlight, wet pearl.

Half terrified, my boyfriend hung the speaker back on its post, then drove us to the end of Campbell. We parked among cholla and ocotillo. I was a little shocked that he had in his billfold a foil packet. Had he been planning this? I was too naïve to notice how worn it was, too young to suspect that he replaced it every few weeks, just in case. His whole gymnast's body was straining, hard, beautiful.

He fumbled the lubricated casing onto himself. Asked if I was sure, if I really wanted to.

World changing, always, that resounding breathless yes.

My Father's Wives #3

Lola was the real estate agent who helped us find the rental house on Malvern after we left Marcia's. It had a pool, but March weather was too chilly yet to let us swim.

Dad came home a couple of weeks later and said, "Lola's going to do our laundry."

Danger. Danger. Danger.

I said, "Dad, can't you just sleep with her for a while?"

Dad said, "With an attitude like that, how's it ever going to work?"

"Dad, she has eight kids. Count 'em. There are four of us. Twelve kids. How's it ever going to work?"

"What do you know? You're just a kid."

And so they married. And my sister Ginny stayed on restriction for the duration. Lola couldn't stand her sassy mouth. Sue spoke only in monosyllables and never looked Lola in the eye. John got caught with cigarettes. As punishment, Lola shaved off his shoulder-length hair. He ran away.

Lola demanded that I shake the gallons and gallons of powdered milk we went through. She demanded that we clean her slum rental units. She demanded half my wages from the Dairy Queen.

That I refused. "I'm saving to go to college."

"You think you're better than the rest of us?"

"No. I'm just going to go to college."

For high school graduation, Lola and my dad gave me an incredibly ugly green suitcase. I took it as an imperative—go, get out. I did.

Deeply guilty for leaving the little kids, I took off.

Higher Education

I thought the university was a place where people read books and exchanged great ideas. Then I moved into the dorm.

Scribe

My college friend Evelia could make words out of other people's feelings. She could write out a letter so loving a young wife back home in the village with her baby could learn it by heart after paying to hear it only once. She could add a phrase, just tilt the words a little, and the novia who got the letter would also get the picture—her beloved was cheating and didn't deserve her.

My Father's Wives #4

Dad's fourth wife, Bobbie, was gentle and long-suffering. She was quiet and shy, but learned to sing so he could get paid for a duo gig at cantinas across the line. She went to live with him in Rocky Point, Mexico, where the drinking never slowed. Once she sobered up, though. She couldn't quite remember what it was about him she found attractive. He accused her of what he was doing—cheating. When she found out he'd used her bank account to hire somebody to follow her, she came back across the line and left him there.

In his version, she abandoned their marriage. Gave up.

Military Ball, 1970

One night when I left my dorm room to get some food, I couldn't get back. Gila Hall was surrounded by protesters, anti-war slogans ripping through the air like heat-seeking missiles. I was afraid of the mob, rocking police cars, turning them over, setting fires along Park. I was mad at the mob, getting in the way of my education, the one I was earning myself nickel by nickel. I didn't want the war over there, but I didn't want this one either. Looters, violent opportunists. Nobody much giving peace a chance. Boys born the same day I was had a high number, weren't likely to be forced into uniform. Boys born on my sister's birthday had a much harder time hanging on to their limbs. The few black guys on campus disappeared. The fewer Chicanos evaporated. The lottery, the deferments, which draft board you faced—none of it was fair.

My friend Andy was head Air Force ROTC cadet at a time when protesters ransacked the ROTC building. He stood by his commitments, an intelligent young man who didn't question his orders. After graduation he was going into a Titan missile silo in the desert, a place where each officer wore a sidearm. If the order came to press the button and one man hesitated, the other had sworn to shoot him.

I told Andy, "If you ever get the order, I hope you refuse."

He said, "If I thought there was a chance of that, I wouldn't go into the silo." He brought me a poster that said the only thing sadder than war was having nothing worth fighting for.

Andy had to find a date for the Military Ball, had to have a young woman in formal attire stand with him in the receiving line. He begged. I told him he owed me big time. It was May, already one hundred and ten degrees. I hoisted my breasts into a strapless dress and pinned up my waist-length hair. Andy came to pick me up in his '57 Chevy with hood locks. At the gala, I watched cadets suffering in full dress, their overheated faces apoplectic against high-collared white jackets. Between handshakes, I whispered, "Why don't you take off your jacket?" Andy was horrified.

"No cadet can do that until the commanding officer does."

I watched that commander, all spit and polish, doing what he thought proper. In a tiny nation in Southeast Asia boys our age were killing and dying. In this room, boys our age were not questioning.

Forever

On a June afternoon in 1974, holding a spray of long-stemmed red roses, I stand before a creepy preacher next to my hiking buddy, Wayne. We decided on Tuesday, gathered a few folks on Saturday.

It is terrible, what I'm thinking. He is a good person, precious to me.

If that preacher starts talking about forever, I'll bolt.

Map

My young husband and I rode a BMW motorcycle to visit family in California. Grandpa Moen loaned us a map. We tried and tried to find the road along the river, two-lane blacktop winding through the valley. Then we checked the date on the map—it was fifteen years old, and charted a place that existed only in people's memories or imaginations. Mission Gorge Road, the trees, the river, had given way to freeways, concrete, houses. Where my mother rode horses as a girl, gone. Visions buried under subdivisions.

Poway

The old joke ran in the family—that Grandpa Howe couldn't wait to meet his Maker. God, on the other hand, had all the time in the world. Grandpa Howe wouldn't drink smoke dance watch movies play cards curse miss church laugh at a coarse joke. Grandpa Howe wouldn't shake hands with a Catholic. (Catholics and Communists were uniting to take over the world.) Grandpa Howe wouldn't take girls to church unless they wore modest dresses. We learned early to wear shorts to his house. Grandpa Howe wouldn't drink a drop of the liquor folks on his mail route gave for Christmas. He boiled it into nasty cough syrup. Grandpa Howe wouldn't stop, even when Grandma said, "Now, Phil."

Even so, I wanted my young husband to see, to know, wanted to try to say hello. We rode a BMW motorcycle Grandpa admired without saying so.

My father told a story about working at a filling station—sixteen years old, saving for a Harley. The owner told him to tidy up the asphalt out back. He swept it all, hosed it down. Driving out, he saw a lady's nylon caught on the spigot by the john. Stuffed it in the trash bag on the gearshift. His dad's Olds, heavy as a tank, he drove straight home.

That Sunday, he faced the Board of Deacons. The inquisition decreed he'd sinned, or held sinful thoughts, or held in his mind if not his hand contents of said stocking. He told his story again, in the quiet voice that meant *watch out*, but they sentenced him to three extra hours of church each week till he learned obedience.

He never willingly set foot in church again. Conversation with his father strained. His mother, pained beyond speech, told him with her eyes, *You're a good boy*. But she couldn't talk back to the old man.

Even so, I took my new husband to meet them, pointed the way to their cottage in Poway where whitewashed rocks half-circled the drive. Grandma had picked butter beans and chard, new frills of lettuce, roasted a hen she'd raised from scratch, poked tines of a dinner fork through white cake so dissolved cherry Jell-O would marble through.

In the kitchen Grandma told me she always held to her own beliefs, I should too. A man can take all the breathing room. Don't let him. She said that with a grin, stroked my face ear to chin. Then we brought the food out to our men.

Silos

After growing up with Titan missiles planted all around my town, I moved far north, where there's nothing strategic (besides the pipeline) to bomb.

Then the Star Wars folks dreamed up ways to spend money we could have used to teach people to read. The systems they've tested have flunked. No matter. They've gone ahead and planted missiles at Fort Greeley, Alaska, and aim them toward whatever threats they identify or invent.

My Father's Wives #5

Connie, his fifth wife, translated for the whole community when shady real estate deals threatened everybody's beach shacks in Mexico.

His fifth wife taught me to make tamales, both ways—the way for those you'll sell and the way for those you'll serve.

Dad flies remote-controlled airplanes out in the desert. When insomnia hits, he puts on headphones and takes in all-night conspiracy theories and right-wing hate jabber.

Connie has decorated with lace every surface of their trailer. Now, in his seventies, Dad's finally at peace. At least he seems at peace.

∞

Dad said to me once, "Each time I got married I thought I was making things better for all of us."

Could he have believed that?

I don't think even he believes it any more.

∞

Connie told me that Dad said he did his best to see that his kids had a mother. She said, "I told him you should have made sure they had a *father*."

The Natural State

Growing up, I saw many ways marriage could be used as a weapon.

In college, I learned all the rhetoric about patriarchy, how marriage keeps women dependent and makes children into chattel.

When I broke apart my marriage, sacrificed eleven years of shared history, I was broken too, so damaged I couldn't breathe.

I lived for more than a decade unattached, wary, not letting lovers too close.

When I met Joe, he soon asked, "When should we get married?" I stared at him. "Marriage *is* the natural state."

Stunned, I said, "And you've just arrived from what planet?"

Holy Man, 1992

Once, on the island of Kauai, a woman took me to a Buddhist ceremony. We stopped first at some cabins left from the time sugar cane was a major crop. We gave a ride to two women who lived in the fields.

In a modest house, we gathered. The brass bowl sang. The altar held rice, oranges, a handmade scroll. After chants and meditation, the holy man who had traveled far to be there asked people what was in their hearts. A few people spoke, and he spoke back, calm, patient. He talked about spiritual vibrations loose in the world, as real as radio signals. We cannot hear them until we tune in. But they're there, as surely as air.

I trusted him.

I asked how I could help her, my mother who didn't want to be here.

He bowed his head, waited. Then he said quietly, "A child can atone for her mother's death wish."

He did not say how. I did not ask.

It was a great gift, this possibility.

My mother had been twenty years in the ground. No matter.

At my best moments, I tune in.

Twenty Questions

If she had lived, would my mother suffer macular degeneration, and hold books close to her face in the small slice of vision left to her?

If she had lived, would she with great effort (like my sister) have quit drinking?

Would she have gone to college finally in her fifties?

Could she have lived, as she wanted to, a life of the mind?

Would she have traveled to Norway to find her roots?

Would she have found a partner who loved to dance?

If she had lived, could she answer our questions?

If she had lived, could she answer her own?

Had she lived, would my mother have written out her angers, burned them in a ritual so personal even smoke took her side?

Would better medicines have allowed her to breathe?

If she had lived, would our bonds to her be weaker?

If she had lived, would she have opened her fists to find the words she needed?

Had she lived, would we make her pay for what she did?

Would we offer her second, third, fourth chances?

Would we bite her back?

If she had lived, would we gather for Thanksgiving dinners? Would she make the fruit salad and pies?

If she had lived, would she have cared for her parents as they faded, grew old, died?

If she had a dotage, would her hands palsied by Parkinson's tremble toward her great-grandchildren?

Given time, would her list of joys have stretched longer than her list of torments?

If she had lived, could she have loved us?

Handicapped

Even after her diagnosis for congestive heart failure, Grandma Moen resisted. She didn't want that blue placard with the stick man in the wheelchair. Didn't want it dangling from the rearview mirror.

"Other people need those spaces worse than I do," she told me.

"You get out of breath walking from the kitchen to the living room," I reminded her. Hard changes—she'd moved from the house where she and my grandpa raised their kids, the house where in one year she got news of the death of her first

born, my mom, and news of the death of her own mother. Her husband died while they lived there. The mulberry tree he planted on their twenty-fifth anniversary now spread its canopy over the whole front yard. She'd been facing the attrition of old age, friends slowing down one by one, curling into arthritis, their memories chipped away by Alzheimer's. So many friends dying that she stopped going to funerals. She'd send a letter to the family, but no more funerals. She'd made twenty years earlier arrangements with the Neptune Society for her ashes to be scattered at sea. No ceremony.

Her own memory was fine, her wit intact, sharp as ever.

"I'm not handicapped," she said.

"No," I assured her. "Just not quite mended. What about if you use the spaces until your breathing calms down, okay?" She agreed to the compromise mostly so we didn't have to talk about this any more.

We headed out for her favorite Mexican place, a little storefront where a woman about her age stood all morning patting out by hand fresh tortillas, turning them on the big comal using just her quick fingers. I pulled the car over the outline of the little blue guy confined by his wheels, went around to hold her hand so she could balance until she planted her quad-tipped cane.

∽

I had years to prepare for Grandma Moen's death. I took a sabbatical and spent a year with her as my eighty-three-year-old roommate, listening to her, loving her, helping her up each time she fell. We laughed every day. I gave her the hard news that she couldn't live alone any more, it was just too dangerous. And still when her time came I was useless, not ready. I dove so deeply into denial, I didn't come to her deathbed when she called.

∽

Handful of ripe mango heavy with juice I balance, guessing where to slice so the knife might just scrape by the face of the pip.

If I guess wrong she will forgive me anyway, grandmother offering stories for breakfast.

Making a Cake

FOR HARRIET MOEN

> I thought, It is simple to be a man,
> simple to be a woman if we love
> what is brief, what is given to us,
> and clear the gloom with it.
>
> MAURYA SIMON

It was a day unlike any other. We stood at the counter mixing up a box cake for cousins due soon. I reached behind me for the scraper, and you let go, fell straight back on the floor. Already, the edges of your mouth whispering blue little words from before or after language. I knelt, afraid, and held you while tidal waves washed through you, then grabbed the phone, called for help.

Did I fall down?

Yes, be still.

Did I fall down?

Yes, don't worry.

Did I fall down?

It's all right. I'm with you.

Did I fall down?

Yes. You'll do anything to get out of making a cake.

The whole length of your body shakes, helpless laughter you won't remember.

Did I fall down?

&

Paramedic whirl dumped peaches and cherries fruit bowl basin catching thin yellow gruel your body wracks up paramedic whirl IV gurney. Did I fall down? What medicines? Clear airway for oxygen, your muscles given over to the power of rescuers, the dignity of the one who allows them to rescue, bare need consuming this paramedic whirl utter tenderness of firefighters lifting you, their big hands. How the one wiped your mouth after you were sick, then held his palm against your cheek, your barely upholstered bones.

∞

Somewhere between the blood-spattered kitchen and the blood-spattered emergency room your glasses, tucked between your fingers by the ambulance driver, slipped away. So when your questioning grew past Did I fall down, and you could once again fish up from the depths your last name comma first you wanted to see. Again I could not help you.

The edgy resident panicked at a low number and nearly did a salty number that would have dispatched you forthwith. But a brisk teaching nurse pretended to explain things to her new charges, let the shaky doctor know that for a CHF patient three percent sodium's a cocktail more potent than Molotov's.

∞

On your side, you asked when we would go home. The young doctor prepared sutures to crazy quilt the bad spot overripe on your noggin. All mush back there, old age's fontanel, your quick brain so full. Throbbing intricacies of how you're put together altogether beyond this man and yet . . . And yet I'm grateful for his stitching, I whose sewing never came to any good.

When they wheel you in to do the science fiction cross-section head scan, you quip, "What if it comes up empty?"

∞

In the ward the brusque efficient one goes to yank off the IV anchor, an adhesive ankh on your forearm. Careful, I warn, but she's already torn your tissue-skin.

Your blood, my tears, and she sees us right then finally as human, runs to find the paper tape she'd said they didn't have.

∞

When you closed your eyes calmly and breath entered and left you calmly, I left you in the care of people for whom you are no miracle. I went back to your kitchen. Wiped up the place your head had been. Wiped up the scattered spray. Pouring ruined cake batter down the sink, I noticed the fruit bowl, carefully rinsed, turned upside down to dry.

∞

In front of you the Home Health nurse we like asks, "What happens if one morning you go in and find her . . . not breathing?
    I feel our air go small. Stunned, I look to you.
    Your eyes say, *Search me*!
    Guess I'll cross that bridge knowing there is no way to prepare.

∞

No way to know yet the new kind of loneliness that will be in the world without you. Knowing we share our greatest sorrow—in a long life yours outliving your first born, your only daughter, the child who grew into the teenager who carried me. In the world without her, how to live. Simple as the gesture of brushing a baby's hair, simple as the gesture of brushing an old woman's hair. In the world without you.

∞

Walking with you in painful sunshine out to get the mail I rest with you three times, point out inca doves, hibiscus, lilies of the Nile. Beside the natal plum, I hold your bare arm, crushed velvet, magic wand.

∞

Every night the wound opens, spills onto your pillow reminders of the body's ingenuity for betrayal, the constant surprise of pain constant but unpredictable. After your shower I soak the dried patch holding washcloths over the soft spot. Out of the wispy hairs I strain gently the used discarded blood.

Then the good part—I part your baby fine hair, arrange it out of the way of the healing place, stroke your warm scalp, let touch take over, a genuine laying on of hands, over the odd knob made odder, over the perpetual upstart of your brain, over the secrets told and kept, the things we have not confided but share anyway, you and I, stroke longer and longer, longer than it takes, until you turn to me and smile, beatitude beyond language and I pronounce you gaw-juss and we laugh, ready to take on whatever this day has to give.

The Inside Story

FOR HARRIET MOEN

Slathering the probe with ice-blue gel, the technician captures
in cross hairs the suspect vein, gasping, open, a gray mouth sur-
facing. Grainy as an old Philco, sound reveals the inner secrets
along your inner thigh to the naked eye. *See, it should collapse,
compress, when I hold it down.* He shows me what it should do, how
it should act then grows quiet when the vein-lips stay parted,
practicing like a young girl for her imagined first kiss. So gentle,
his glide, so serious, his glance. You relax against his steady hand
except where odd chunks of cells will not allow, little knots that
perplex the flow, that stop short your great-grandson who blurts,
"What's a blood clock, Mom?"

I wonder this myself, clock and clot, how we measure start and
stop, the ebb, the flow, blood ties that bind more securely than
unreliable time.

Forty-five years—how lucky!—our lives have overlapped,
passed-down stories bleeding one into another, colors deeper
with each telling. The thrum of blood will carry on in new
thighs, new lips, not ours—but because of ours, a richer shade.

Stubbed Toe

Josefina, hired to be with you every moment while I work my job far away, whispers that you never get dressed anymore till today but today yes because I was coming.

I bite back tears, and scoop you up, so light! How is it possible that you, pure rock, could turn to a wisp? Dandelion fuzz that one breath, invisible, could scatter into the beyond. Your barely covered skull, bowed. You can't stay still in the big chair, you want to be in bed. In bed, you call to walk around. Turning the marathon, hall to kitchen to living room, you brush softly your small toe along the molding.

Crumpling in pain, you cry real tears and chant, "I've got to get out of this situation, I've got to get out."

Stupid with grief, I say, "Your toe barely touched . . ." and you chop me off with eyes fierce as cleavers.

"What do you know, lady?" You tell me you're not putting on that oxygen any more, you can't stand it touching you.

I whisper, "You don't have to. It's okay. We'll just keep walking."

Timing

So lucky, Joe and I, to find one another later in life. Timing *is* everything. We spent most of our lives getting ready for one another. For years we were aware of one another, vaguely, in the way people notice folks in other circles. We got acquainted when Joe was scheduled to receive an honorary doctorate at University of Alaska Fairbanks for his years of service and support. I was selected to receive a faculty award his family endowed. My friend who runs the UA Museum gave a dinner party. She called and asked, "Could you sit by this guy and just talk to him? Pleeeeze?"

"Sure," I said. "But you owe me."

There at Aldona's table Joe and I started talking. We haven't stopped.

Taking Care

On our second date, Joe asks if I want to go with him to a dinner at the university chancellor's house. Fairbanks is a small town. I'm not sure I want our business quite so soon on the street.

"People are gonna call me a gold digger," I warn him.

"People are gonna call me a cradle robber," he smiles. "At least while they're talking about us, they aren't doing anybody any harm."

∞

Aldona says, "Maybe your grandmother stuck around until she knew you'd be taken care of."

Grandma dies the same year I find Joe. Joe helps me grieve for her.

Chatanika

We drive north up the haul road.

High, the Chatanika, high this year, surges the flats, soaks the valley. Chatanika spreads wide where gravel braids. Where banks snug close, where rock, earth, and root gang up, high water scours, carves, its own image changeable. Chatanika, in pools deep green, in eddies steeped tea, freezes and thaws, makes its way on, full of grayling flashing like thoughts among the millions of mirrors at Minto.

What brought me exactly here?

Is my flowing through the world a fit gift?

Have I nourished more roots than I undercut?

∽

What gets away—the hours, the days. Our best fish stories we repeat not for what happened, but for what they let us invent. We forget lots of things with good reason, lots of things for no reason. We let loose of things we want to reel in. The nature of the soul—what we have inside that we can't get to. And what we keep, quiet.

∽

What about what we can't forget? Even when we want to . . .

∽

On the way over to the Echo Lab, I picture Tyrolean ravines, snowy mountainsides and crisp air, voices thrown as if the world were playing catch with us.

But this is Palo Alto. We drive through Stanford's medical campus, park, and walk through Boswell. Where's Johnson? The rules for the test say NPO for six hours prior. So I haven't eaten or drunk since we had good Indian food last night. In solidarity, Joe fasts with me.

My appointment's at 9:00 a.m. This whole thing should take fifteen minutes. Fifteen minutes, and we may have a better idea of the origin of clots that caused the small infarcts, the places in my brain deprived of blood until they died.

The neurologist here, Dr. Tong, says my chart and my abilities do not match, that he had expected more disability. I do not understand quite how the brain rewires itself, new sections taking over the duties of the injured ones, but I'm walking proof that this happens. Anyway, fifteen minutes, and then we'll go to the Barn and find something easy on the throat.

For some reason, we need some coded labels before we can pass go. We go to the desk and ask for some. We're told to wait. We do. Nobody else is there, and the clerk doesn't seem to have any work to do. We wander the halls, trying to find someone else. After a long wait, the second clerk sends us around the corner, back to the first desk.

Apparently going to the other desk is a faux pas beyond forgiveness. The clerk will not acknowledge us. Finally we just stand at her counter. When she gets off the phone I tell her that we're not going away until she deals with us.

By the time the rude clerk prints our labels and we've waited again in the hallway, it's close to 1:30. We are cranky. We're beyond peckish and into the realm of ravenous.

∞

The technician brings us into a little room right off the main corridor. He's genial and calm, confident. He introduces himself, Kendrick, and explains that I'll need an iv, for a mild sedative to control the gag reflex, and so that once they've got a good look at the heart, they can put bubbles in, to watch how they move through the chambers. Bubbles? Don't bubbles kill people, or cause strokes? I guess they know what they're doing, so I don't bolt. But I'm not quite as relaxed as I was.

Kendrick slides an ultrasound tool iced with blue gel between my breasts. We watch the mitral valve as it splays and pulls back, its spikes agile, fast. That mitral valve, sea creature fathoms below the surface, sustaining human life.

My own strong heart, in black and white, a classic. Colorized red and blue flashes go with the flow, as Kendrick shows me auricle, ventricle, aortic arch. This view is pretty good, he says, but the echo will show things much more clearly, without the interference of flesh and bone. All it has to travel through is the esophagus. Kendrick hands me a wad of tissues to wipe off the gel.

∞

An RN, Heidi, comes in to start the IV. I warn her that I'm a hard stick, and she says, "Not to worry. I'm good at this." I lie back, and will my veins to welcome the needle. Her fingers prod the crooks of both arms, but can't rouse a likely suspect. She slaps the back of my right hand. Harder. Says, "A little poke." Then she jabs around beneath the skin. After a little while, she sighs. "Sorry."

She soaks towels in hot water, wraps both my arms. After a few minutes, she tries the crook of my left arm. No go. She wraps it back, and tries my left hand.

"You *are* a hard stick." Well duh. Probably I'm a little dehydrated, but I can't drink now. So my vessels retreat even more than normal. She tries the right hand again. Sharp poke, then zow, she hits some nerve. Hot electrical pain slices between my fingers. Ow. I allow myself to say ow.

She says, "Just relax. Pretend you don't mind this at all." Her probes feel like the blade of a pocket knife.

"Ow," I say, louder.

"I'm so sorry," she sighs. When she removes the needle, a black bubble begins to rise across the back of my hand.

"See, I did find a vein," Heidi says. "You're gonna have a hematoma." She presses down, as if trying to stop the flow.

Kendrick says, "Do you think we ought to get Rina?" and Heidi nods. He goes out. She wraps my arm back up. She leaves too. Joe comes close, and touches my face, my shoulder.

They come back with an anesthesiologist. Rina's on a trauma. But this doctor's good. He hits blood and gets it to flow back on the first try. Just as we're celebrating, my body takes it back.

He says to Heidi, "I always slap, to get the veins to rise up." He tries the back of my left hand. Nothing. He grimaces at the spreading bruise on my right. He turns it over, tries the wrist. This poke burns. Bad. Finally, he says, "Usually I give it three tries, and then acknowledge my limits. But we could try your jugular."

I have no desire to have a needle in my neck. Perhaps this shows, because he says, slightly put off, "I do this for a living. You'd have nothing to worry about." Easy for him. He goes out. I ask Kendrick if we can do this echo without the IV. He says he'll ask, but it isn't best, and he's never seen it done without one. So the doc comes back with a new set of needles, slips one into my neck, and plows around. After several years, Heidi says, "Yea!" They shoot something through to make sure the line's working.

The doc asks me to open my mouth wide, but to hold my breath. He warns me he's about to spray the back of my throat with something to deaden it, and I don't want this spray in my lungs. I open up, hold my breath. He picks up a bright yellow pressurized can with a little metal tube sticking out, like a can of WD40 with the straw in place. He sprays. Gack. Turpentine. Fumes sear my eyes and nose. Kendrick hands me tissues. Again. They have me swallow a double finger full of gel viscous as hair-setting goop. Then they ask Joe to step outside. I don't like it that they lock the door after him.

I have to lie on my left side, facing away from the monitor, careful not to crowd the IV in my neck. Kendrick puts down a pad to catch the drool. The doc threads down my throat a cable the size of my thumb. "Breathe deeply, steadily. If you feel your-self wanting to gag, just breathe deeply. That helps."

It does. They push and pull till the probe's just right, talking over me as if I were not present. My throat closes a few times. I feel like a cat with a long slick hairball. Whatever they've given me makes me leaden, as if my body were cut out of dentist's aprons. Kendrick asks the doctor to confirm what he's putting in the report. They watch bubbles going in.

"Bear down now," Kendrick says. "Again . . . okay, you can stop." They debate. "Medium?" "One millimeter."

223

After twenty minutes, they pull the tube firmly out. The doctor goes. Joe comes back.

Kendrick says my heart looks good. No new clots. No apparent damage. He tells me we all, as fetuses, have a hole in the ventricular wall, so blood can move freely between chambers of the heart. Before we have to breathe, this is efficient. In most people, the hole closes right after we're born. In maybe thirty percent of adults, it stays open. I have a one-millimeter hole, which opens whenever I tense my abdominal muscles. Usually this isn't a problem. But if a clot occurs, in the leg, say, it can push through the heart and travel quickly to the brain. So this hole puts me at a medium risk for more strokes.

I croak thanks. My throat feels freshly grated. The Xeroxed sheet of instructions tells me I can sip cool water. After a few hours I can drink. If that stays down, I can eat. This does not feel likely any time soon. I'm not to operate heavy machinery. So how do they expect me to maneuver this body? Joe keeps his arm around me, through the hallway, over the brick walkway. He grabs a snack to eat in the car, offers me some. Nothing looks worth the pain of swallowing.

∞

Out front, everything's in bloom. We admire the overblown roses, their extravagant aromas, rainwashed.

We head north, past the city, to a place where hawks dive among grapevines. A few vineyards still bear blue clusters, but most of the harvest's gathered. Leaves pile up. The sun's low. Great swaths of purple and yellow sweep uphill toward tall madrona, their deep red bark the color I carry in my throat.

∞

The echo isn't by a long shot the worst procedure I've endured. Why does it stick with me so vividly?

Maybe because it can. Maybe I hold on to it because this much I can recall.

∞

How many of us get a look at the workings of our own hearts? And when we do, via machinery or meditation, love or trauma or art, what do we make of what we see?

Can we stand it?

Not for long, I suspect. Not for long.

A hole in the heart.

A hole to live with.

SIX

∞

Mi Corazón

If I had written a personal ad for a mate, I wouldn't have described Joe. He's an engineer by training, a miner by trade, a businessman, a pilot, a scuba diver. His family mines the coal that produces most of the electricity in Interior Alaska and quite a bit in Korea.

Politically, we often disagree. Neither one of us can spout our easy assumptions any more. We have to think. We have to respect opinions we don't share.

I have to think through my suspicion of mining. He asks me to picture the alternatives in Alaska. Rivers stay frozen for seven or eight months a year, at the time when people use the most energy to heat their homes. Wood heat works for people with the time and inclination to cut and split wood and to feed the stove. But if everybody used it, the boreal forests would disappear. Solar power? How well would that work when the sun in deep winter shows up for three and a half hours a day? (Yes, as a duplicate system, it works well in summer.) We have wind in some places, but no machinery dependable enough to harness it at forty below. Oil and gas are more expensive by far than low-sulfur Alaskan coal.

"Okay," I say. "Okay. Thanks for the electricity."

Joe laughs.

Steward

A life-long Alaskan, Joe has the attitude that you don't foul your own nest. He has been doing reclamation at the mine for twelve years, shaping disturbed earth, then broadcasting from airplanes a mix of indigenous seed to slow down erosion. School kids collect cones and plant seedlings of new trees until willow and scrub can reinvade.

No wonder he is offended when a government regulator who has never visited Alaska shows up and tells him how things must be done.

Appliances

At my log house among the birches out past Ester, I've made a life. Lots of books, students, potluck dinners. Joe enters my world, watches me spread wet clothes on wooden racks near the furnace instead of stuffing them in the dryer. Watches as I luxuriate in plunging aching-cold hands into warm soapy dishwater—too few plates for a noisy load. He tells me, "Know what? You have a really uneasy relationship with your appliances."

He's right. Machines I don't really trust. When I get a new computer, Joe can't wait to put it together. If I'd let him, he'd take it apart too.

"Don't you want to know how it works?" He's exasperated.

I really don't. "I want to know *that* it works. Then I want to go to work," I tell him.

My mistrust of machines shows up again when Joe introduces me to scuba diving. Joe understands intuitively how each piece of gear fits together and works, even the pieces that are new to him.

Joe fiddles with the custom housing that will protect his video camera under water. Double checks that his space-age Dick Tracy wrist computer is offering accurate readings.

To me, it's a great puzzle, this universe. When we get something to work, I say, triumphant, "It's magic!" Joe says, deadpan, "It's physics."

I've done the bookwork, sure that if my life depends on simple arithmetic done sixty feet under water, I'm sunk. I'm glad to have a computer on my wrist that figures out exact depth, bottom time, PSI of air remaining, proper speed of ascent, surface interval, and time that should elapse before flying. I bet my life on a regulator, a tank, the compressors that mix the right blend of nitrogen and oxygen.

I learn how to attach my regulator to my tank, how to check and double check the mixture of gases that I'll breathe, how to signal if I need help. I've never needed until now to control my buoyancy, to try to fly straight and level at the proper depth. I learn to add and subtract air from my buoyancy compensator to keep my place in this underwater world. Doing all the arithmetic called for in the charts, charts designed for young Navy Seals, I realize how little they apply to me, a woman in her late forties. I estimate conservatively all my bottom times, all my safety stops, all my surface intervals. The computer cries out when I've sunk too low, when I've ascended too fast.

Strapped into all this new technology, I'm miraculously naked in the ocean. Overloaded with gear, overloaded with information, wide-eyed, ready, I'm at home as soon as the water closes over me.

Dive

Above, a quilt of molten glass, the surface of time liquid, each breath suspended, rising in capsules, CO_2 gleaned from my blood. Below, desire to know how soft corals open themselves to night, how parrotfish sleep in slick cocoons, how shape shifters escape, eight arms through any exit, impossibly tiny, jagged, close. Below human need, invisible trails of sound echo whale to whale, echo through oceans of time. Below the surface, barnacled keels, dwarf volcanoes sharp as lava, below the cinched zodiac, the archer, the target, the zen letting go. Below arrows of barracuda, whole quivers shot. Below hard surge bashing lava loose, below the betrayal of sabertooth blennies posing as cleaner wrasse, then biting. Below wrecks of commerce or war, wrecks of pleasure sunk into sand, below artificial reefs laid in brine, heated by lava flows, hatched in air—the internal weather of ocean inside us.

Decisions, Duress

My aunt Suzie was young when copious bleeding made doctors recommend removing her womb. She had wanted more babies, but lupus wouldn't let that happen. So they took the uterus, but left her ovaries, healthy and pumping out estrogen. Twenty-five years later that decision haunts.

Suzie's had more reason than anyone I know to want to leave this life. She's never quite out of pain.

Lupus paralyzed her, and doctors told her she wouldn't walk again. She learned again the intricacies of how the spaghetti gets onto the fork, how the fork trembles up toward the mouth, how the mouth chews, how the throat swallows. Then she concentrated on walking. She told me, "I just want to see my son grow up."

Twenty years later, she can walk a few steps unaided, from the fridge to the stove, for instance. A motorized scooter gives her back a good measure of independence—she can tool down to the grocery store, or get a prescription filled on her own. (She only dumps the scooter over now and then.) The computer widens her world. Suzie corresponds with scores of people, her all-caps messages letting us know that this afternoon three hummingbirds dive-bombed the feeder. Her e-mails use the oddest punctuation, a question mark at the end of almost every sentence? As if nothing is settled, and everything up for discussion? As if nobody can be sure of anything? But that she wants to see what comes next? Every blessed day? Every painful hour? Every precious breath?

∞

A strange disease slowed Suzie down. She couldn't understand what her body was doing. It hadn't betrayed her before.

Misdiagnosis and potent mis-medication made her kick holes in the walls, lash out at Harry, and fear that everyone she trusted was out to get her. Harry found her outside naked, trying to get away.

After dozens of doctors had tried, one finally identified lupus as the culprit. By then, though, wrong amounts of wrong chemicals had damaged her brain stem. She couldn't walk, feed herself, get dressed.

Doctors advised Harry to put her in a nursing home.

Instead, he sold her share of the bakery, closed his business, and set about easing her way as much as he could.

Green Sea Turtles

By the pinnacles, effortless oval shadows skim over us, ease into place at the cleaning station, where yellow tangs and saddle wrasse feast on sea lice, scour algae out of grout lines between the turtles' tiles. Vigilant eyes close. A tangle of black durgeon triggerfish whirls, dust devil of fish. Parrotfishes' sharp beaks chip coral into their mouths. What their bodies can't use builds the beach. I picture the beach, far off, where the turtle we're watching will scoop her nest, push from her body great masses of unbrittle eggs. Those long-clawed fins will cover over the cache, and she'll return, an upturned cradle rocking in surge, to arch her pebbled neck so lithe blue and gold wrasse can nibble beneath her shell's collar.

Breath heavy as turtle shells strapped to our backs, we immerse ourselves one brief hour in the larger world we seldom see. Whale calls miles out bound in. As if on cue, the fish as one swarm a new arrival. The abandoned turtle looks both ways, crosses the path of our bubbles, biting in case some might be jellyfish, then rises to sun herself as long as she likes at the surface.

No Way

First lupus, then ovarian cancer. What makes my aunt Suzie, who has lived all her adult life in an unreliable, pain-wracked body, unable to comprehend suicide, much less consider it?

No matter what it contains, she wants each day.

∽

Suzie's the wife of my mother's brother Harry. Mom was oldest, Jack second, then Dan. Mom wanted a sister more than anything. When her parents brought her another brother, she wouldn't look at him. She refused Harry.

Weeks later she held him, and their friendship began, special always because she had denied him.

By the time her fourth brother, Kris, showed up, she had stopped hoping.

Snowflake Eel

The snowflake eel clamps razor teeth tight in the tail of the mahi mahi carcass fast turning pure bone. Beneath the ledge, braided in and overslung, two white-mouth morays, two yellow-head morays, one zebra eel yawn in warning. They've drawn the discarded skeleton (long as a human) close in, stripped clean what the fisherman's quick filet knife left behind. The snowflake, discontented with picked-over ribs, levitates, mouth tight in the tail, exposes a cubit of wrist-thick self. With a pit-bull's frenzy, the eel shakes the bones so hard the luckless spine lashes like a knotted whip. The yellow margin on top can't sneak his tail in edgewise, free swims just enough to nudge the bones back under lava. Larger and stronger, the big morays cast the snowflake a look, then gnaw the few trailing shreds washed in on the light surge of evening.

Bakery

Before she was sick, Suzie worked hard at her family's Italian bakery, the Masiello Bakery, filling cannoli with ricotta and chocolate chips, then dipping the ends in chopped pistachios. Each hollow eclair she impaled on a tube, then eased it off, pumping the crust full of custard. Jess napped on a pallet in the storage room behind the ovens. Mr. Masiello laughed out loud when somebody asked for his recipes. "Sure!" he boomed. I asked about that—why would he give them away? "Even if they know the ingredients, they can't do what I can do." That was the truth. I watched his deft hands, patting slivered almonds onto the side of a layer cake, one revolution, four pats, and the cake was covered. Suzie stood close to the master baker every year of her growing, learned his skill, shared his great laugh. They insisted on the best—best ingredients, best pastries, best breads.

One time Suzie and I stopped to get liquor for the bakery. Rum, to be brushed on split layers of cake with a four-inch paint brush. Kahlua for the mocha flavors. Beers for the guys after work. Some lowlifes started following us as we walked to the cashier—"Oooh, ba-bees, where's the par-tee?"

∞

On the Big Island of Hawaii, I pushed Suzie's wheelchair up to where lava had flowed across the road. We watched plumes of steam and acid and fine particles of glass rise up where the volcano was creating new earth. Suzie, too, created new earth, earth we can stand on to see better, earth we can plant to grow food, earth we can explore, following her example.

Camouflage

We've been told not to kneel even if the sandy paths between outcrops of lava look inviting. That's where crocodile eels disappear. And anything that will let you touch it, don't. This I remember unsteady in deep water reaching to brace one hand and several tons of gear—then I see, quick and terrifying as any epiphany—the rock's eyes steady on me. Titan scorpionfish. This ambush hunter, original still life, suspends time. My eyes trace the great square jaw, each stripe of fin, the toxic spines flattened to blend with red algae. Vital disguise, his life depends upon being mistaken for stone. And mine, at this moment, upon being not more than one breath from my buddy, shaking his dive light, trying to catch my eye. Who are we down here, out of reach of usual language? Translating every gesture of beings better adapted to be here, we suck our finite air, some of us calm as parrotfish wrapped for the night in self-made cocoons, some of us skittish as red-speckled octopi, remaking our shapes each moment, each breath.

Glacial Erratics

Suzie's tumors—what are you, swelling there? Stones rising from spongy tundra, old moraine, stones thrown by motion, specks of silt caught catching others, the gathering gravid, the odd spawn beyond gestation, no bearing on eros, no touch of loving other, no gift of seed, just gravity so gritty the ovaries catch on, battered boxers in a clinch, hanging on as if this last embrace holds in its very shape the peal of absolution, bloody ablutions, cheers ... No body's saved by this bell.

Dive Log

Ninety feet down we spy blue ribbon eels, planted under shelves of coral, wavering in the surge, their yellow mouths coughing open.

Every time I dump air out of my buoyancy control device, every time I let lead weights draw me down, I find life I never imagined. Some of my best childhood moments I spent conjuring, I thought, this. But that desert kid sitting on the bottom of the deep end, holding her breath as long as she could, didn't come close to this richness.

Close to the surface, nurseries for damselfish, orange and purple, their fins trailing long as princess costumes. A little deeper, stinging anemones with clownfish snuggled down immune among the tentacles. Lower, red sea fans sway over giant clams slamming shut as they sense us near. Down below, a forest of corals and sponges, animals impersonating plants. At the slightest touch, bright blue and red and white Christmas tree worms no bigger than thimbles flick back into their holes. A gobi zips up and down the strand of wire coral where it will spend its life.

We hang on to a shallow bommie and manta rays swoop over, feeding on plankton. Close enough to touch, six-foot spans of manta, the prehistoric curls round their mouths. We don't touch, knowing that one finger drawn along their surface removes a layer that protects them, one touch opens them to infection.

Crown-of-thorns starfish, too many. For its gorgeous shell, the trident trumpet has been hunted almost to extinction. It's the only thing that finds delicious the spine-studded crown-of-thorns. The trident can slip its foot under the star, avoiding all its weapons, and flip it onto its back, exposing the juicy under-side, a glistening loaded banquet plate. Without this predator, the crown-of-thorns star has taken over, eating so much coral the reef can't sustain itself. For miles some places, all that's left is bleached reef skeletons and more hungry stars.

Trying to Tell Me

One afternoon when we were alone, Suzie said, "I've struggled for *so* long."

"I know," I said.

Truth is, though, I know very little of her hardships.

I held her until she let go. Her body was massively swollen from steroids and other drugs, her arms a patchwork of bruises. She let her bald head rest on my shoulder. I tried to encourage her, "At least your CA-125 numbers are heading the right direction."

"Yeah," she said, unconvinced. Then she just looked at me, for a long time.

No Right Word

I wonder how many ways I failed her. She might have been trying to tell me that she wouldn't be here long. I might have eased
her way a little by saying, "When you're ready, you can go. The
family will watch out for Harry and Jess." I didn't.

I knew we didn't have much time left.

I thought we had more time.

Wake

I hop the red-eye and fly all night from Kona to Los Angeles. It's not quite real that Suzie won't be there. I wait for my brother's flight from Tucson, and we drive to Orange County to be with Harry.

Numb, I pick up refreshments for the reception, help him with the details of the funeral. Harry asks me, "As the family wordsmith, will you speak at the ceremony?"

Of course.

Maybe one reason I survived was to speak words to honor her. I say to the crowd, "We all have inside us favorite pictures of Suzie. Here are a few snapshots I'd like to share with you."

Suzie, during chemo, cooking supper for handicapped kids in the group home down the street.

Suzie, rising from her wheelchair to dance at her son's wedding, the son doctors warned her she'd never live to see grow up.

Suzie, breaking into an impish smile when John Howe said, "I was shivering like a mutt shitting a peach pit."

Suzie, fitting together pieces of a jigsaw puzzle. Harleys, castles, horses and the reflections of horses, hot air balloons, meadows, farmhouses . . . Puzzles. (The only one she ever abandoned was a puzzle I sent her of three cherries, surrounded by little candy dots you sprinkle on cakes. The outside edge was irregular, and the background all the same. After the cherry one, she wrote, "What did I ever do to you?")

Suzie, calling as she pushed her walker, "Can I help?"

∽

W. S. Merwin writes:

> Every year without knowing it I have passed the day
> When the last fires will wave to me
> And the silence will set out
> Tireless traveller
> Like the beam of a lightless star.

The poet wisely does not offer advice or lessons to be learned. Instead, he points out what we all know we don't know—the anniversary of our death.

We know that day for Suzie now, a day each year to remember her, without grief if we can. Beyond suffering, we hope. She has shed her body, that ill-fitting disguise, shed the odd costume of this life. Knowing this anniversary, we open ourselves to larger mystery. Next and next and next, if there is a next. Plunge into the unknown.

Good Dream

After she's gone, it's a good dream when Grandma Moen talks to me, tells me stories, a good dream when I go to the mailbox and there's a letter with her familiar elegant handwriting. I dream I answer every letter she ever sent.

Dear Gma,

In my dreams we roll out a wide rectangle of dough, dot it with butter, spread thick brown sugar and cinnamon. We roll it into a stubby anaconda, then slice clean spirals, mandalas set to rise again under clean dish towels. You perch on the two-step kitchen ladder, the ash on your Marlboro defying gravity, while we boil a couple of double yolk eggs to munch with the fresh buns.

I remember how your face fell, landslide into a canyon we couldn't see the bottom of, when you stepped out of the jetway. You'd come to bury your first born, my mother. You knelt as if I were still a toddler, and I staggered, sixteen, blind, into your embrace.

Somewhere in all your stories, through all my life, did you slip me the secret sign we'll use to know each other on the other side? Will I remember it, if you did?

Or will we mingle in the aroma of cinnamon and yeast, rising up to feed anyone (earthly or not) who hungers?

Love,

Los Muertos

On Día de Los Muertos, people set up altars to welcome back those who have gone before. In the Sonoran desert, where the dead are said to cherish fragrances, paths of marigolds help the ancestors find their way.

It's not mournful at all. Music, singing, dancing, a candlelight vigil. Huge spreads of food. After the dead have tasted their favorite dishes, living people feast on homemade tortillas hot off the comal. Husky tamales—meat, green corn, sweet. Skull-shaped candies, breads, cookies. The gritty bonedust of panocha. Saladitos turn every mouth into a watering hole. Fry bread starts out flat, then puffs in hot oil, its emptiness honeyed.

∞

El Zarco Guererro, Carmen de Novais, and their band Xichanindio play música in the park. Zarco has made wild, haunting masks for all the musicians, skull faces for all the dancers. I take my nieces Amy and Melanie. Just the right age for swings and slides, they celebrate staying up late, revel in being outside after dark. They aren't embarrassed to dance with me.

Barefoot, we dig tiny graves with our toes as we dance with all those who've gone before. Then, during La Mascarada, the procession of ritual masks, Melanie turns around. She takes one look—sees horns and fur and bared teeth—and takes off running. We find her crouching, terrified, behind a little wall near the swings. I gather her onto my lap and hold her, her bony little butt digging into my legs. She nestles, warm against my chest, just about calmed down.

The band takes a break, and our friend, still in costume, walks over to show her she doesn't need to be afraid. He lifts the mask and smiles.

"IT'S GOT ZARCO!" Mel wails, ready to bolt.

∞

On the altars, pictures of loved ones out of reach. Loved ones forever the age they were when they left. Tokens of lives. A fishing lure. Skate key. Spurs. Carved *bate* for frothing hot chocolate. Pierced earrings. Locket. Dancing shoes, size tiny. A lizard-skin cowboy boot, planted with jumping cactus. Calavera candles flickering.

Calacas—Skeletons riding motorcycles, getting married, having babies. Skeletons at typewriters, skeletons on the rollercoaster. Skeletons playing billiards, every ball on the table a skull. Calacas riding horseback, their holsters flapping. Calacas playing cello and violin, the tune just beyond our hearing.

Kitchen Table

Once I wrote a poem about the death of my mother, not a pretty death, not an easy poem. Before I sent it out into the world, I wanted to show it to my grandmother. This was a woman who had already survived her parents, two sisters, her husband, and now her first born, her only daughter. I did not want to cause her more pain. We sat together at her kitchen table, the one she and my grandpa bought used back in 1942, and we leaned against the morning glories painted on the chair backs. She lit a cigarette, and let the ash grow, defying gravity, while she read the poem. Again. I was beginning to worry, afraid that I had, without meaning to, done her harm. She sat quietly for a while. Then she said, "We did not know the same person. I knew her from the time she was an infant. You knew only the troubled adult. So we'll never see her the same way. It would be wrong for us to."

We talked most of that night, close in our separate ways of seeing. Neither one wrong. That moment taught me, as a writer, as a teacher, as a person. Each mind, each imagination, must have its own slant, must have the confidence to take on the world in its own way. What has stayed with me strongest from that night was the mutual respect, the love, for other ways of seeing.

Second Chances

Ginny once mused, "Look how my life is just like Mom's—I have four kids, three girls and a boy, I live in Tucson with a musician, I have a boxer dog." She's pleased by this.

I shiver in the heat, and think to myself, *Who would ever ever ever want to replicate Mom's life?*

Only years later do I realize maybe she's trying to do it all over, do it better. Maybe she's trying to get it right.

I've tried too. My first husband's mother shot herself. In the forehead. On purpose. (Her daughters always called it "Mom's accident." I guess they had to call it that.) When Phyllis came out of intensive care and out of the psych ward, she came to live with me and Wayne. I was in my first year of grad school, teaching two courses of comp, taking two grad courses, treading water. I'd come home and try to convince Phyllis that this was a good day to eat something, a good day to talk, a good day to take a walk around the block.

It didn't hit me until years later, at her funeral—Phyllis took an overdose of pills—that I was trying to do better, trying to get it right. I was trying to save us all, Phyllis, my own mother, us kids, myself.

My simultaneous beliefs—We don't get to do it over, so be careful what you say, what you do, in the first place. Yes, every breath is a do-over, every breath a chance to get it right.

Recorder

Because I know so little of my father's side, I invest in a tiny digital recorder. We test it, prop it on the table between us. At first the questions are dry, factual—names and birthplaces of his parents and grandparents, aunts and uncles, cousins. Then he starts telling me about all the places he's lived in his life, all the work he's done, some of the reasons for the choices he's made over the years.

It's the first substantial conversation we've had my whole life. I'm over fifty years old.

After an hour and half, I ask him with an open heart, "Is there anything you might want to tell me but you've never had the chance?" He's quiet a long time. I say, "You don't have to answer . . ."

He looks at me gently. "No, I have something to say."

He looks down at his hands, folded over one another as if protecting something inside. "I think I know what you're asking."

"That's funny . . . *I* don't know what I'm asking," I admit. His smile's wan. He takes two deep breaths, one for each of us. Begins.

New Wrinkle

They were eighteen and nineteen, married three months, not quite used to sleeping in the same too-small bed. Restless and cramped, they'd jostle each other out of their dreams. She was showing, her belly hardening, getting in the way when they had sex.

Still, it was pretty unbelievable to be grownups, to be on their own. Unbelievable that she'd take off her clothes right in front of him. He was pretty sure his mother never did that in front of anyone. But Hanna would be talking about some kid dropping water balloons off the wooden roller coaster at Mission Beach, waiting to ascend the highest arc, then bombs away, dropping the sleeveless eyelet blouse she'd worn a few hours, still curved like her for a moment, then collapsing into mere cloth. She'd keep talking as she reached behind her back to release the hooks and eyes of her bra, cotton spirals on each pointy cup thrust toward him. He felt himself sink in, hypnotized. Then the miracles, the splendor of her breasts shining, light caressing them mysterious as mother of pearl, then in his mouth, so warm, her nipples leaping, alive.

She lay awake one night, the full moon casting long shadows. Her turning woke him, and he propped himself on one elbow to look at her. It was still hard for him to fathom that they were husband and wife.

"I have something to tell you," she said. She took a deep breath.

He could tell that he didn't want to hear this, didn't want to know. He looked out the window, clouds drifting past the pockmarked moon.

"It's not easy for me to tell you this, but I think you deserve to know." She spoke softly, her chin tucked toward her chest. "Johnny, look at me. Please."

He brought his eyes up to meet hers, feral in the moonlight.

"The baby I'm carrying might not be yours."

∞

Stunned, in shock. For days, he drove his forklift on automatic pilot, lucky he didn't drop pallets of airplane engines on some poor soul.

What should he do with this knowledge? It tangled up inside him, cut off his air. He couldn't stand to think of her . . .

If the baby wasn't his, why should he be a sucker? Maybe he should cut and run. He didn't really want to be married anyway. He had a lot of living to do.

He opened the throttle on his Norton, cranked it back all the way, felt salt air tangle his hair. What did he know about being a father? His own dad went to work, did his route and a little extra, then went to work for the church. He had nothing to do with his kids.

But maybe the baby *was* his. It could be, easily. There wasn't really any way to tell. It wasn't the baby's fault.

Raising the kid would be no different than adoption, no different from giving shelter to an orphan.

How could he ever trust Hanna again?

Maybe he wouldn't.

After days with his stomach aching, he decided. He'd stay. He'd stay, but keep his eyes open.

She slobbed around the house and didn't even comb her hair. She cooked nothing. One day he came back to get the lunchbox he forgot and found Hanna dressed real pretty, on her way out.

Not Knowing

It would explain a lot, if my dad were not my father. I don't look much like my siblings, who are tall and blond. What if he isn't? Is there some stranger in his seventies who helped put me on this earth? All our lives would have been different if my mother would have chosen him. Why didn't she? Did he ever even know she had missed her period?

If my dad and I do in fact share DNA, the distances, the absences remain.

I'm curious. How would we react if we confirmed his paternity? How would we be if we learned that his whole life changed because of an egg he didn't fertilize?

Precipitous

Like rain in the desert, squalls over ocean, clouds caught on mountaintops until water gathers itself into heavy drops that rain down slanted to dry earth. My birth.

As the first child of a very young mother, I was expected to take my time, to make her labor hard and long. Instead, I was right there, ready, willing to surf the great flood gushing out from around me, as if knowing no ocean would ever again be so private, shared only by us two.

Kus-sun-ar

Caribou stew. Thai food. Lasagna. Cakes. Homemade loaves and soups and covered dishes. Glen Simpson brings salmon he caught dipnetting all night at Chitina. He used needle-nose pliers to nip out all the invisible bones. He stays to tell stories. Growing up at fish camp, he'd sneeze. Tahltan elders would say, "Kus-sun-ar!" Otter. They invoked otter's name to wish him close to one who lives in more than one world. Otters are shaman helpers, on land, in water. Glen tells me how otters live inside women, curled up just above the stomach. This feels true. I feel my otters, restless, disturbed.

He tells me how powerful shamans make their kit bags from otters. I'm living this story. I'm an otter, skinned in the round, my pelt pulled off in one piece. Stitched into a kit bag, I feel the shaman placing his healing tools one by one into my emptiness.

✂

I think of all I know that isn't available to me anymore. It's there some-where, but won't rise to any bait. What should I use to fish? What should I be happy to leave circling in the depths?

✂

Because Joe's a prominent citizen in Alaska, our wreck gets more than normal coverage in the media. In the first accounts, I'm listed as Joe's wife. This so offends one of my colleagues at the university that he calls the *Fairbanks Daily News-Miner* and reminds them that I have a whole identity of my own, as poet, professor, person. The next account mentions a person closer to the one I recognize as my self. Among the injuries they keep listing is a "small skull fracture." Guess it's small when it's not your skull.

The front tire of Joe's bike, now the shape of a fortune cookie, is the real star—it shows up in color in the newspaper and on television. We become poster children—first for surviving, then for advocating for bike path safety. Joe's appalled by the apathy. Department of Transportation officials say their priority is high-ways, and in tight budget times bike paths get the dregs. The police say that catching people on four-wheelers is really dif-ficult, so they don't pursue them. Great message, eh? They could make the same case for not solving murders. Even the head of the local bike club, who could use this spotlight to talk safety, sighs and says motorized vehicles show up all the time on the paths, so try to stay out of the way.

Multiple use—walkers, moms with strollers, rollerbladers, cyclists. I'll go this far. But no four-wheelers, no motorcycles.

In the winter, skiers. And skijorers towed by dogs. But no snow machines. This is the law already.

Joe and I advocate to the borough assembly for an ordinance that says any motorized vehicle on the bike paths can be confiscated. We try to get the message out that if you make your machine into a weapon, you forfeit it. The assembly thanks us for our comments.

Every time I see a kid on a four-wheeler on the streets, on the bike paths, I want to pull my car in front of him, get out, show him my scars. And the bare headed people on bikes make me crazy and sad, especially the kids with helmets hanging off their handlebars.

After three months: The DOT has not cleared the sight line and hasn't repaired major potholes in the path. The police have made a good faith effort to keep kids on four-wheelers off the paths, and to catch the scofflaws, but haven't caught many. One assembly woman has sought out public comments on bike path safety. No action from the borough so far.

After a year and three months: the same.

Maybe some good won't come of this.

∞

A friend I see once a year has not heard about the wreck. Pensive, he says, "Okay, so we've published books, won prizes, taught for years. But do you ever get on yourself, and say, 'So what have you done *lately*?'"

I laugh, and tell him my questions this year have been more basic: Will I breathe? On my own, off the ventilator? Will I see clearly? Will I walk? Will I read? What does it mean to be alive?

Then I think about people all over the globe without medical care.

∞

I've begun to think through how it applies to me, the fact that death could come at any moment.

＊

Joe claims that in the hospital I would be talking in a normal voice, having a regular conversation. Then the phone would ring. If it were one of my relatives far away, I would put on a high-pitched, weak "little girl" voice to let them know how hurt I still was.

I deny this still, didn't do it, never happened.

Joe says that after one of these moaning conversations, my brother called the nurse's station and had Joe come out of the room. John wanted reassurance that I was in fact recovering, because I sounded so puny.

It's not surprising that a person might whine a little to her family, or that she might use her voice to show what her body feels. But I didn't do that, didn't "put on," didn't, didn't, didn't.

And even if I did, why does it matter so much to deny it?

＊

A year and four months after the wreck the Victim Coordinator calls to invite us to an Emergency Detention Hearing. D. is in trouble again. I tell her that I really thought our wreck had given him a wake-up call, and she tells me, "Some people take longer than others to wake up."

Being treated with compassion hasn't taught D. much. I wonder what he'll learn in jail.

＊

I think about how much of the world comes to me through my eyes, all the life on the river I'd miss out on if someone yelled, "Look!" and I couldn't. Two beaver pulling out on the far bank. The smudge of pink along the edge of green aurora. My great-great-grandpa's handwriting on letters written during the Civil War. The shape of poems, their sound and rhythm on the page. Joe's face, turning to me in the morning. Joe's face, turned to me in the night. My own body, stumbling, perplexed. My own body dream-flying in a Pacific current, floating by batfish and barracuda, floating by bommies alive with soft coral.

∞

Joe and I started the year 2000 in a magnificent way—scuba diving in Fiji. We saw forests of vivid soft corals, many white-tipped reef sharks and gray sharks, and one eight-foot leopard shark, just lounging on the sandy bottom. Red sea fans swayed in the current. The dive master, Pele, showed us a rare ghost pipefish, which we'd never have seen without her help.

Then in June, our lives got tossed like dice.

Short version: We got in a bad wreck, but we're healing.

Long version you already know. It took courage for that young doctor who made the decision to give me the risky drug. She got to be heroic, and I got to breathe. By myself, off the ventilator. Every doctor I've met since then (seems like hundreds) tells me I'm lucky to be alive. I can just hear my grandmother, Harriet Moen—"Hey, if you were THAT lucky, you wouldn't have gotten hit."

∞

It was an afternoon splendid as the cover of a seed catalog, better even, because it sprouted on its own, a volunteer, wild gift.

It was my turn to choose where we'd ride. So I suggested, "Let's do Farmer's Loop, on the bike path where it's safe."

Joe swears nobody else notices. It still drives me crazy when a word gets away. Sometimes a word I've used since I could talk eludes me, a word simple as *oatmeal* or *milk*.

Sometimes an abstraction plays hide and seek. Often I can describe the concept—"You know, when you contribute to your own destruction . . ."

Much later, after the conversation has flown by but I've kept searching for the word, my brain offers up *complicity*.

It's odd—I always assumed I'd get old. And now I can't be sure. So Joe and I wake each morning happy to be alive, glad to be together.

Balance is less trustworthy than it once was, but much better than it has been these last few months.

I can do most things I want to do, only slower. My memory is still full of blank spots. (Joe says, "Your memory wasn't perfect *before* the wreck, you know.")

"Skittish and annoying" might describe me when I'm the passenger in a car now. Joe says if there's a brake light visible anywhere, I yell, "STOP!"

My energy visits and stays a while sometimes.

My gratitude has never had so much exercise.

Injuries to my lungs mean my New Year's dives were my last. It hits with a pang now and then that D. has taken the oceans away from me.

On better days, I resolve to become a great snorkeler. It's not so different—most of the world I can't see from my one small vantage point.

I'll look to Stan Waterman and other great underwater videographers, and to writers and poets to bring me to the depths.

∞

In "The Purpose of Altar Boys," Alberto Ríos writes:

> Tonio told me at catechism
> the big part of the eye
> admits good, and the little
> black part is for seeing
> evil—his mother told him
> who was a widow and so
> an authority on such things.
> That's why at night
> the black part gets bigger . . .

For me, the pupil of one eye stays always the size it will be for the rest of my life. So I guess I let in good and evil equally, at least in one eye.

High Tide at Useless Bay, September 2001

No crash, tremor, shudder of sand or breaking wall of water, no warning in the air.

Just one morning, they're there—fugitive raft of logs cut long ago, chained together, then broken, lost, stranded in salt. Sodden gray, jumbled trunks. Rusted chains too big for human hands bind them.

A long time floating, this brace of logs.

We cannot walk here as we did before.

November, Día de los Muertos, Whidbey Island

To celebrate that we are not among them, we choose Day of the Dead for our first post-wreck ride. We air up the tires, strap on our helmets, take deep breaths. Balance is still tricky. I can't quite tell what's flat and what's not, can't quite tell when my foot will touch ground. Extra dark sunglasses give my eye a break—when one pupil doesn't react, sunshine hurts.

I force out of my mind visions of falling, visions of me and the bike tangled in blackberry brambles, visions of cars swerving but not missing. Every muscle in my body is on alert. It's as if I have to give orders for each motion.

The focus this morning reminds me of the day I got glasses, after a childhood of seeing blurry. Each blade of grass stands out, distinct. Each chip of gravel, each glint of glass. To mount, I lean my bike so far over the pedal touches. Joe holds me steady while I balance on one foot. My right leg, the hurt leg, clears the hurdle, fishes a moment in midair, finds the pedal. I straighten, balance, breathe.

I look both ways, outside, inside. We push off, wobbly, into the rest of our lives.

IN THE AMERICAN LIVES SERIES

Fault Line
by Laurie Alberts

Pieces from Life's Crazy Quilt
by Marvin V. Arnett

Songs from the Black Chair:
A Memoir of Mental Illness
by Charles Barber

Out of Joint: A Private and
Public Story of Arthritis
by Mary Felstiner

Falling Room
by Eli Hastings

Hannah and the Mountain:
Notes toward a
Wilderness Fatherhood
by Jonathan Johnson

Local Wonders:
Seasons in the Bohemian Alps
by Ted Kooser

Bigger than Life:
A Murder, a Memoir
by Dinah Lenney

What Becomes You
by Aaron Raz Link
and Hilda Raz

Turning Bones
by Lee Martin

Thoughts from a
Queen-Sized Bed
by Mimi Schwartz

The Fortune Teller's Kiss
by Brenda Serotte

Gang of One:
Memoirs of a Red Guard
by Fan Shen

Just Breathe Normally
by Peggy Shumaker

Scraping By in the Big Eighties
by Natalia Rachel Singer

In the Shadow of Memory
by Floyd Skloot

Secret Frequencies:
A New York Education
by John Skoyles

Phantom Limb
by Janet Sternburg

UNIVERSITY OF NEBRASKA PRESS